HOUGHTON

California
Science

Interactive
Text

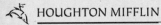 HOUGHTON MIFFLIN   BOSTON

Printed in the U.S.A.

ISBN 13: 978-0-547-00465-5
ISBN 10: 0-547-00465-6

17 18   0877   19 18

4500700688

Contents

Cells

WHAT DO YOU KNOW?

List one fact about each of these topics.

a. The parts of a cell _____

_____

_____

b. How cells make and use energy _____

_____

_____

c. How cells are organized _____

_____

_____

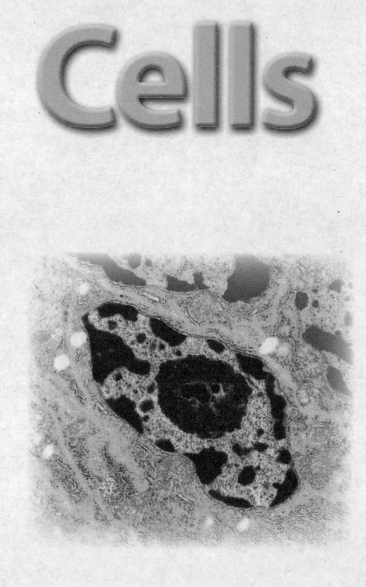

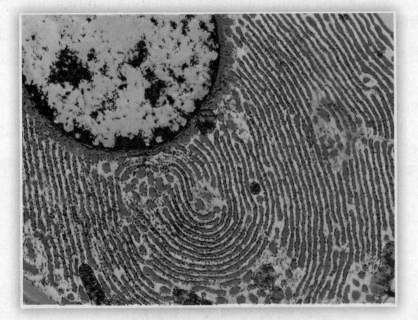

Contents

KWL

WHAT DO YOU WANT TO KNOW?

Skim the pictures and headings in this chapter. List one thing about each of the topics.

a. The parts of a cell _____

_____

_____

b. How cells make and use energy _____

_____

_____

c. How cells are organized _____

VOCABULARY

cell the basic unit of all living things *(noun)*

cytoplasm gel-like material located between the nucleus and the cell membrane *(noun)*

nucleus the cell part that contains DNA and directs cell activities *(noun)*

organelle a structure that performs specific functions in the cell *(noun)*

VOCABULARY SKILL: Word Origins

A microscope is a tool that scientists use to study cells. The word *microscope* is a noun that comes from the Greek words *mikro*, meaning "small," and *skopos*, meaning "spy" or "watcher." What is a microscope?

_____

_____

_____

1 What Are the Parts of a Cell?

Cells are the building blocks of all living things. Cells have parts that move things around.

The Cell Theory

The part that makes up living things is the **cell**. All living things are made of cells.

Most cells are too small to be seen with the eye. Cells were not discovered until the first microscope was built.

All living things, even caterpillars, are made of cells.

2.a. Students know that many living things have structures to transport materials.

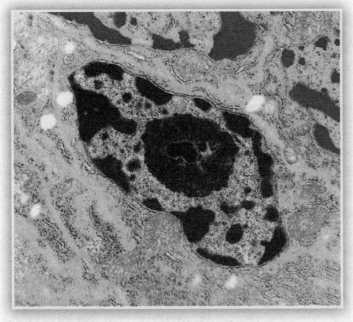

This image shows the nucleus of a nerve cell magnified.

Scientists are people who study our world. Scientists studied cells and came up with the cell theory. It says:

- All living things are made of one or more cells.
- The cell is the basic, or most simple, part of a living thing.
- Cells come from other cells.

Today, there are new ways to study cells. Scientists are learning more about the way cells work.

1. List the three parts of the cell theory.

a. _____

_____

_____

b. _____

_____

_____

c. _____

_____

_____

2. Use the Venn diagram to compare plant and animal cells.

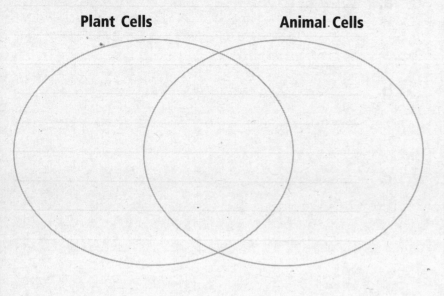

Plant Cells   Animal Cells

What Cells Do

All living things need to make or take in food. Living things need a way to take care of and protect their bodies. They also need to grow and reproduce, or make more living things of the same kind. They need a way to get rid of waste, too.

Some living things are made up of a single cell. That means that one cell takes care of all the needs of the living thing. Other living things are multicellular. This means they have a lot of cells.

Comparing Plant and Animal Cells		
Need	**Plant cells**	**Animal cells**
Energy source	Sunlight, for making own food	Other living things, eaten for food
Support and protection	Thick cell walls and fluid-filled cell parts	Cell membrane and other parts
Growth and reproduction	DNA and proteins	DNA and proteins

The cells of a living thing that is multicellular cannot live apart from each other. They work together to take care of all the needs of the living thing.

Some cells have different uses in different kinds of living things. But all cells do some things the same. All cells make copies of themselves using a molecule called DNA. Most cells also have the same kinds of parts.

Cells of animals, such as fish, are different from cells of plants, such as algae.

3. List four things that all living things do.

a. _____
_____

b. _____
_____

c. _____
_____

d. _____
_____

4. What is the difference between a cell that is part of a multicellular living thing and a cell that is a single-celled living thing?

_____
_____
_____
_____

5. What do cells use to make copies of themselves?

_____

6. What is an organelle?

_____

_____

7. The left column of this chart lists the jobs that are done by organelles in the cell. Fill in the right column by writing the name of the organelle next to the job it does.

What the Cell Part Does	Name of the Cell Part
Stores DNA	
Helps a plant stand up	
Lets wastes out of the cell	
Holds all the other organelles	
Directs what the cell does	
Lets food, water, and gases into cell	
Provides hard outer layer to protect the cell	

The Parts of a Cell

All plant and animal cells have even smaller parts called **organelles**. Each cell part has its own job to do for the cell.

Nucleus The **nucleus** (NOO klee uhs) directs what the cell does. It stores DNA. How a living thing will look and act depends on DNA. DNA is passed from parents to their young.

Cell Membrane The cell membrane is a thin covering that is around all kinds of cells. It lets food, water, and gases in and lets wastes out.

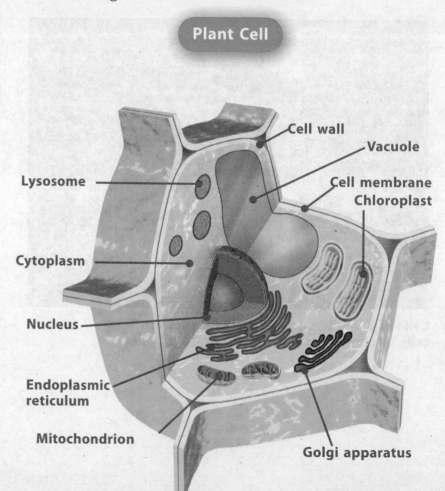

Plant Cell

Cell wall
Vacuole
Lysosome
Cell membrane
Chloroplast
Cytoplasm
Nucleus
Endoplasmic reticulum
Mitochondrion
Golgi apparatus

A plant cell has an outer layer called the cell wall.

Cell Wall Plant cells have a cell wall. The cell wall is a hard outer layer that is around the cell membrane. The cell wall protects the cell. It helps the plant stand up. Tiny holes in the cell wall let things pass in and out.

Cytoplasm Between the nucleus and the cell membrane is the **cytoplasm** (SY toh plaz uhm). The cytoplasm is a thick liquid. All the other organelles are in the cytoplasm.

I Wonder . . . If a plant cell has a cell membrane around it, why does it also need a cell wall? What would plants look like if their cells had no cell wall?

_____

_____

_____

_____

_____

_____

8. Which organelle gathers proteins and has no membrane?

_____

9. Tell which organelle is found in animal cells but not usually in plant cells. Explain what this cell part does.

_____

_____

_____

10. Why are proteins important to cells?

_____

_____

_____

Ribosomes Tiny ribosomes are found all through the cell. Ribosomes do not have membranes. They make proteins. Proteins make up parts of the cell and they help the cell to do many of its jobs.

Lysosomes Lysosomes are small, ball-shaped organelles that help the cell break down nutrients and old cell parts. Lysosomes are found in animal cells. They usually are not found in plant cells.

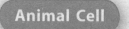

Animal Cell

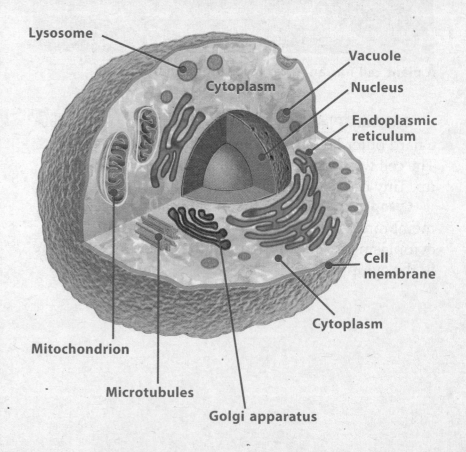

Lysosome

Vacuole

Cytoplasm

Nucleus

Endoplasmic reticulum

Cell membrane

Cytoplasm

Mitochondrion

Microtubules

Golgi apparatus

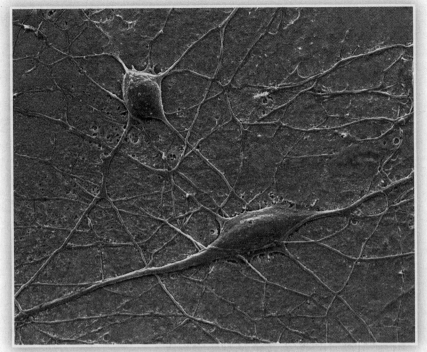
A nerve cell is a special kind of animal cell.

Vacuoles Vacuoles are small bags that have a membrane around them. They are filled with a liquid. They store water, food, waste, and other things the cell deals with. Animal cells may have many vacuoles. Plant cells often only have one.

Golgi Apparatus The Golgi apparatus takes in proteins. It gets proteins ready to be outside the cell. This organelle is made up of many membranes.

11. Use this concept map to list three facts about vacuoles.

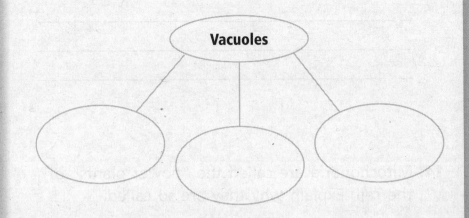

12. What is the Golgi apparatus made up of?

_____

_____

_____

13. What do chloroplasts do? Why are they not present in animal cells?

_____

_____

_____

14. Mitochondria are called the "power plants" of the cell. Explain why they are so called.

_____

_____

_____

15. The endoplasmic reticulum contains many tubes. What is their purpose?

_____

_____

_____

Chloroplasts Chloroplasts are found only in plants and some protists. They have colors that absorb sunlight. Chloroplasts use energy from the Sun to make food. Energy is the power to make change.

Mitochondria These large, peanut-shaped organelles are known as the "power plants" of the cell. Sugars break down inside the mitochondria. Then they let off carbon dioxide, water, and a lot of energy.

Mitochondria are found in both plant and animal cells. The number of mitochondria depends on how much energy the cell needs. If a cell needs a lot energy, it will have a large number of mitochondria.

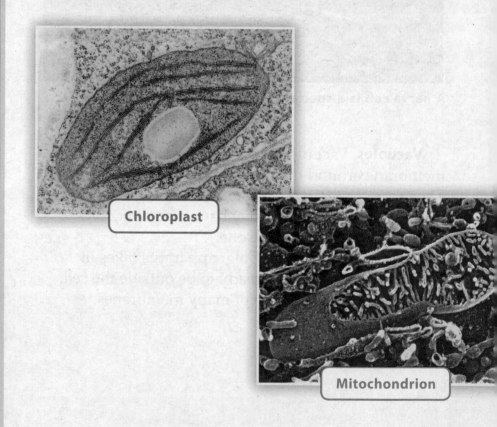

Chloroplast

Mitochondrion

Endoplasmic Reticulum The endoplasmic reticulum (ER) has many membranes and tubes, or pipes that move things. The membranes turn their way through the cell. They have tunnels through which things can pass. There are two kinds of ER. They are called rough and smooth. Rough ER is dotted with ribosomes, but smooth ER is not.

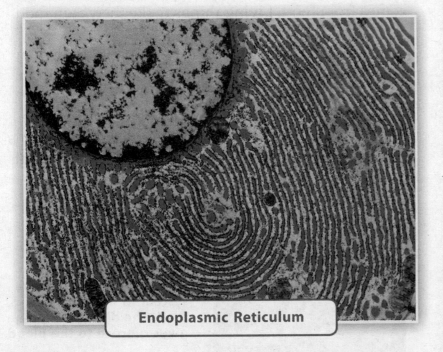

Endoplasmic Reticulum

Summary All cells carry out basic life processes, such as using energy and moving materials into and out of the cell. All cells have similar parts, called organelles. List four organelles that both plant cells and animal cells have.

1. _____

2. _____

3. _____

4. _____

Compare and Contrast How do the functions of a cell in a single-celled living thing compare with the functions of cells in a multicellular living thing?

Single-celled living thing   Multicellular living thing

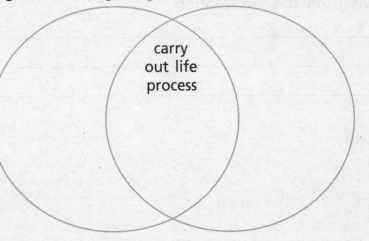

carry out life process

COMPARE AND CONTRAST

How do the functions of a cell in a single-celled living thing compare with the functions of cells in a multicellular living thing?

VOCABULARY

cellular respiration the process in which cells break down glucose in plants and animals *(noun)*

diffusion a process that spreads substances through a gas or liquid *(noun)*

osmosis a special form of diffusion that works to keep water inside the cells *(noun)*

VOCABULARY SKILL: Word Parts

The word *transport* consists of the prefix *trans-*, meaning "across," and the root *port*, meaning "to carry." Write your own definition of *transport* based on this information.

_____

_____

_____

2 How Do Cells Make and Use Energy?

Plant and animal cells break down sugar to get energy. They give off water and carbon dioxide.

Glucose

All living things need energy to stay alive. Energy comes from food. Living things make their own food or take in food from the outside.

Foods can look and taste very different. But when food is broken down, the energy it gives comes from just a few molecules.

The most important molecule is glucose. Glucose is a sugar. Animals cannot make their own glucose. This is why all animals need plants for food. Some animals eat plants. Others eat animals that eat plants.

A koala uses its digestive system to break down food. The digestive system gives glucose to the blood.

2.a. Students know that many living things have structures to transport materials.
2.g. Students know how living things break down sugar to get energy.

Cellular Respiration

Cells use glucose for energy. Animal and plant cells also break glucose down in **cellular respiration**.

Cellular respiration changes glucose and oxygen into carbon dioxide gas and water. This also gives off a lot of energy. The cell traps the energy in a molecule called ATP. ATP is like a battery for the cell. The cell breaks apart ATP whenever it needs energy.

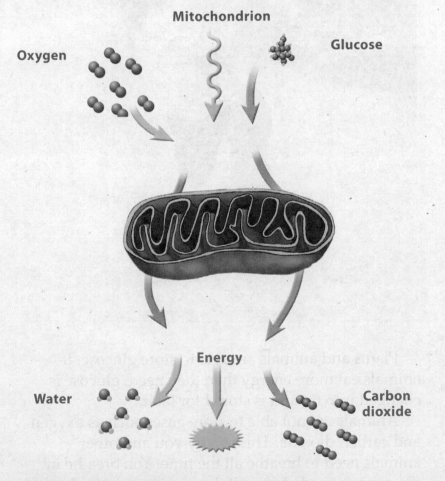

Mitochondria perform respiration in both plant and animal cells.

1. What is glucose and where does it come from?

_____

_____

_____

2. Complete the diagram to describe cellular respiration.

Glucose and _____ enter a mitochondrion.

Cellular respiration changes them into _____ and _____ gas.

When this change occurs, a lot of _____ is given off.

I Wonder . . . If a plant can make its own glucose, why do plants carry out cellular respiration?

_____

_____

_____

_____

_____

_____

3. Why is it necessary for animals to breathe?

_____

_____

_____

Breathing oxygen is a part of the process of respiration.

Plants and animals are able to store glucose. If animals eat more energy than they need, glucose is changed into fat and is stored for later.

Animals are not able to store gases such as oxygen and carbon dioxide. This is why you and other animals need to breathe all the time! You breathe in the oxygen needed for cellular respiration. You breathe out carbon dioxide, which your body does not need.

Why Cells Need Energy

Cells need energy to stay alive. Here are four things cells do to help living things survive:

Making Proteins All cells make and use proteins. Proteins allow cells to be in charge of the chemical reactions inside them. Other proteins give the cell shape and hold it up. Your skin, nails, and hair are made from proteins.

Movement Muscle cells can get bigger and smaller. When this happens, the body moves. Movement takes a lot of energy, so muscle cells have many mitochondria.

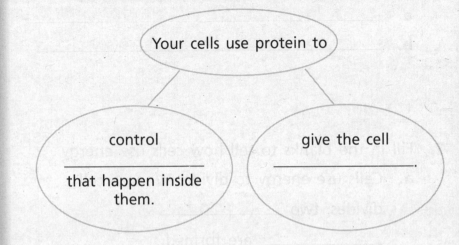

Making Proteins and Movement

Making Proteins
- controlling cell reactions
- providing structure and support

Movement
- moving from place to place, or within the organism

4. Use this graphic organizer to show why proteins are important to your body's cells.

Your cells use protein to

control _____ that happen inside them.

give the cell _____.

5. How do muscle cells make your body move?

_____

_____

_____

6. Identify two ways in which cell division is needed by the body.

a. _____

b. _____

7. Fill in the blanks to tell how cells use energy.

a. Cells use energy to divide. When a cell

divides, two _____

_____ are formed.

b. A cell uses energy to move things into or

out of itself. The cell _____ keeps

some things in or out of the cell and lets

some things pass through.

Cell Division New cells form when old cells divide in two. You grew from a single cell inside your mother into the multicellular being you are today. Each time cells divide, they need a lot of energy.

Transport of Materials A cell membrane is around every cell. The membrane keeps some things in or out. It lets other things pass through the cell. Moving things across the cell membrane takes a lot of energy.

Cell Division and Transport

Cell Division
- growing new body parts
- repairing or replacing damaged parts

Transport
- pumping materials across cell membranes

Moving Materials

Cells need water, sugar, air, and minerals to stay alive. Cells make wastes that must be removed. How do things move in and out of the cell?

One way a cell moves things is called passive transport. The cell does not have to use any energy this way. The simplest kind of passive transport is **diffusion** (dih FYOO zhuhn). Diffusion moves things through a gas or a liquid, such as water.

Diffusion also moves things into and out of cells. Diffusion takes things from places where it is very crowded to places where it is not very crowded.

Passive Transport	Active Transport
Cells use no energy in passive transport.	Cells must use energy to move materials across cell membranes in active transport.

8. Complete the diagram below by drawing an arrow to show particles moving across a cell membrane during diffusion. The arrow you draw should show the direction of particle movement.

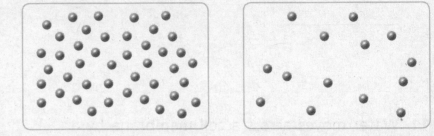

9. Cells have two ways to move materials in and out. Fill in the graphic organizer to tell what those two ways are.

Moving Materials Across Cell Membranes

_____
Cells use no energy.

_____
Cells must use energy.

Complete the sentences to tell how things move into and out of cells.

10. Things move from places where they are crowded to places where they are not very crowded by a kind of passive transport called

_____.

11. Water moves across a cell membrane by a

process called _____.

12. Things move from places where they are not very crowded to places where they are very

crowded by _____ _____.

One form of diffusion is called **osmosis** (ahz MOH sihs). Osmosis takes place across a membrane that lets water pass but keeps out many things that are dissolved in water. Osmosis works to keep water inside cells.

Sometimes a cell needs to move things in a way that diffusion cannot do. This is called active transport. The cell has to use energy in active transport. Things are moved from places where it is not very crowed to places where it is very crowded.

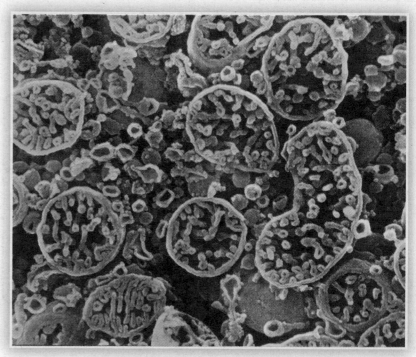

Diffusion and osmosis move materials into and out of cells.

Organisms and Energy

One cell does not need much energy. But an animal made of many cells needs a lot of energy!

Warm-blooded animals with bigger bodies and greater speeds need far more energy than smaller, slower animals.

The need for energy is one reason why many large animals are now endangered, or in danger of not being able to live. When an animal needs a lot of food, it may have to go a long way to find food. The largest animals suffer as people take up more and more of Earth's wild places.

Cheetah

Snake

All three of these animals need energy that they get from food. The cheetah is biggest, so it needs the most food and energy.

Grasshopper

13. What two factors can be used to figure out how much energy a living thing needs?

a. _____

b. _____

14. Rank the following living things by how much energy they need. Use number 1 for the animal that needs the most energy and number 5 for the animal that needs the least energy.

_____ chicken

_____ earthworm

_____ turtle

_____ pig

_____ elephant

Summary   Plant and animal cells break down sugar, releasing water, carbon dioxide, and energy. How does the amount of energy a living thing gets affect that living thing?

_____

_____

_____

Problem and Solution   How does a cell get the energy it needs to stay alive?

Problem	Solution
The cell needs energy to stay alive.	_____ _____ _____

This hippopotamus must find enough food to meet its energy needs.

A plant also needs energy, but not as much as an animal of the same size. Plants get their energy from the Sun. Sunlight makes enough energy for a plant to grow and move things in and out of its cells. A plant does not need energy to move from place to place the way an animal does.

The amount of energy a living thing gets directs how it will grow and reproduce.

PROBLEM AND SOLUTION

How does a cell get the energy it needs to stay alive?

How Are Cells Organized?

Cells join together to do things in multicellular living things.

From Cells to Organisms

A multicellular living thing is made up of more than one cell. The cells work together to do things for the living thing. The cells are specialized, which means they only do certain jobs.

Cells come in many shapes and sizes. The shape of a cell matches its job. Skin cells are flat and close together. This allows them to form a layer that protects the body.

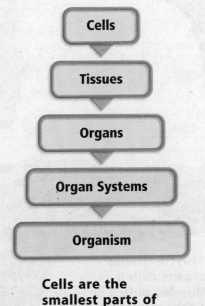

Cells are the smallest parts of an organism.

VOCABULARY

organ a group of related tissues that perform a specific function *(noun)*

organ system a group of organs that work together to accomplish a task *(noun)*

tissue a group of similar specialized cells that work together *(noun)*

VOCABULARY SKILL: Structural Analysis

In biology, the word *specialized* means "adapted to a special condition, use, or requirement." What are some other words that begin with the same letters that *specialized* does?

_____

_____

2.a. Students know that many living things have structures to transport materials.

Add descriptions to the chart to tell how cells are organized.

Tissues: _____
_____

↓

Organs: _____
_____

↓

Organ Systems: _____
_____

Cells are grouped together at different levels. First, they are grouped into tissues. A **tissue** is a large group of specialized cells, or cells with the same job. Muscle tissue is made up of muscle cells.

Together, different kinds of tissue make up organs. An **organ** is a group of tissues that do one job. The heart and brain are organs.

Plants have organs, too. Roots, stems, leaves, and fruits are organs of a plant.

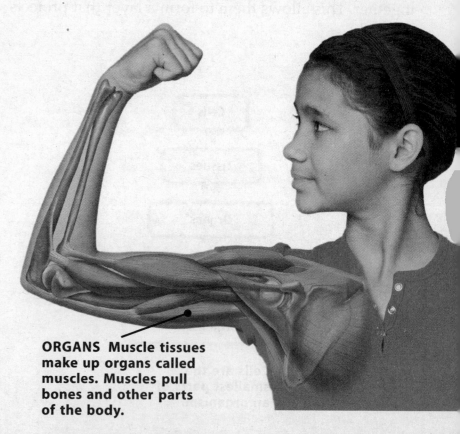

ORGANS Muscle tissues make up organs called muscles. Muscles pull bones and other parts of the body.

Working Together

Organs are grouped into organ systems to meet the needs of the living thing. An **organ system** is a group of organs that work together to do a job. Most multicellular living things have many organ systems.

This diagram shows parts of organ systems for a frog. Plants have organ systems, too. Organ systems work together to keep plants and animals alive and healthy.

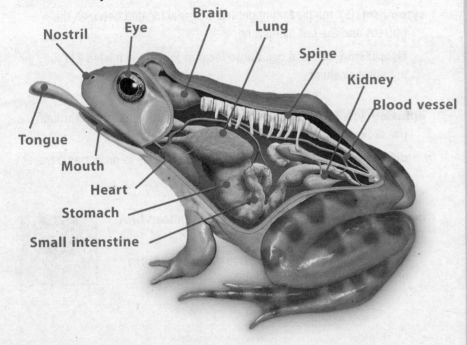

Nostril
Eye
Brain
Lung
Spine
Kidney
Blood vessel
Tongue
Mouth
Heart
Stomach
Small intenstine

A frog uses many organs to keep itself alive and healthy.

MAIN IDEA AND DETAILS

Why do living things need organ systems?

Summary   Cells work together to perform basic life functions in multicellular living things. Write a short paragraph that describes how cells are organized into organ systems.

_____

_____

_____

_____

Main Idea and Details   Why do living things need organ systems?

Organ Systems

Organs work together as organ systems to _____, such as, breathing.

Organ systems help a living thing meet _____, such as, bringing oxygen to cells.

Group two or more of the words in the glossary and explain why they go together.

cell the basic unit of all living things

   célula la unidad más pequeña de todo ser vivo

cellular respiration the process in which cells break down glucose in plants and animals

   respiración celular proceso mediante el cual las células descomponen la glucosa en plantas animales

cytoplasm (SY toh plaz uhm) gel-like material located between the nucleus and the cell membrane

   citoplasma material gelatinoso localizado entre el núcleo y la membrana celular

diffusion (dih FYOO zhuhn) a process that spreads substances through a gas or liquid

   difusión proceso mediante el cual las sustancias se propagan a través de un gas o un líquido

nucleus (NOO klee uhs) the cell part that contains DNA and directs cell activities

   núcleo la parte de la ciélula que contiene el ADN y que controla la actividad celular

Glossary

organ a group of related tissues that perform a specific function

órgano grupo de tejidos relacionados que realizan una función específica

organelle a structure that performs specific functions in the cell

organelo estructura que realiza funciones específicas en la célula

organ system a group of organs that work together to accomplish a task

sistema de órganos grupo de órganos que trabajan juntos para realizar una tarea

osmosis (ahz MOH sihs) a special form of diffusion that works to keep water inside the cells

ósmosis método especial de difusión que sirve para mantener agua dentro de las células

tissue a group of similar specialized cells that work together

tejido grupo de células con una especialización similar que trabajan juntas

 Visit www.eduplace.com to play puzzles and word games.

Circle the word that is the same in both Spanish and English.

Chapter Review

KWL

WHAT DID YOU LEARN?

Vocabulary

❶ (Circle) the correct answer on the page.

Comprehension

❷ _____

_____

_____

_____

❸ _____

_____

❹ _____

_____

Critical Thinking

❺ _____

_____

_____

_____

_____

_____

Think About What You Have Read

Vocabulary

❶ Proteins are assembled at organelles called _____.

A) ribosomes

B) vacuoles

C) chloroplasts

D) mitochondria

Comprehension

❷ What do all cells have in common?

❸ What are two ways that cells transport materials?

❹ Why do complex living things have more than one kind of tissue?

Critical Thinking

❺ A teacher compares your body to a community of people working together. Do you agree or disagree? Explain your answer. What might happen if some cells were no longer able to work together?

Plant Systems

KWL

WHAT DO YOU KNOW?

List one fact for each of these topics.

How plants produce food _____

_____

_____

How plants move materials _____

_____

_____

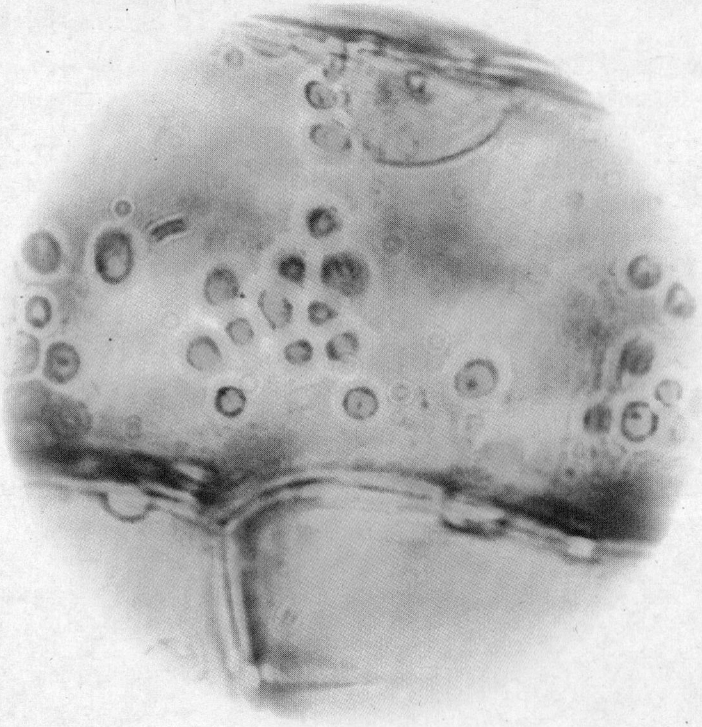

Contents

WHAT DO YOU WANT TO KNOW?

Skim the pictures and headings in this chapter. List one thing you want to find out about each of these topics.

How plants make food: _____

_____

_____

_____

How plants move materials: _____

_____

_____

_____

VOCABULARY

chlorophyll the pigment in a chloroplast that absorbs light *(noun)*

chloroplast an organelle in plant cells in which photosynthesis takes place *(noun)*

grana stacks of membranes inside a chloroplast that contain chlorophyll *(noun)*

photosynthesis the process by which plants transform energy from sunlight into chemical energy *(noun)*

stomata small openings in the bottom of a leaf through which gases move *(noun)*

VOCABULARY SKILL: Word Origins

The word *chlorophyll* comes from the Greek *chloro*, meaning "green," and *phyllon*, meaning "leaf." Use this information to tell what chlorophyll does.

_____

_____

1

How Do Plants Produce Food?

Plants use energy from the Sun to make food. They use water and a gas called carbon dioxide to make sugar. They get rid of oxygen, which is the air we breathe.

Photosynthesis

Plants change the energy of sunlight into energy they can use. This energy is stored in food. Plants do this through photosynthesis (foh toh SIHN thih sihs). During **photosynthesis**, plants turn water and carbon dioxide into sugar. Then plants give off oxygen.

Animals depend on plants for energy. An animal eats a plant and uses the sugars for energy. A larger animal eats that animal and gains the energy first stored in the plant.

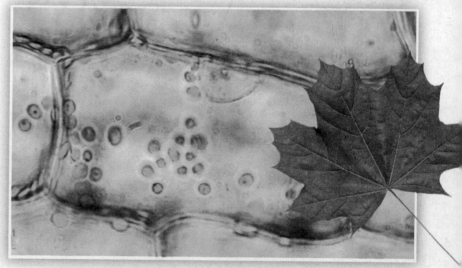

Plant cells have chloroplasts. Light energy is changed to chemical energy in chloroplasts.

2.a. Students know that many living things have structures to transport materials.
2.f. Students know how plants make food and release oxygen.

The green color of these leaves comes from the chlorophyll inside the chloroplasts.

Photosynthesis takes place in organelles called **chloroplasts** (KLAWR uh PLAST). Most chloroplasts have the same shape and form.

Each chloroplast has two membranes around it. Other membranes wind through the inside of the chloroplast. These membranes look like flat bags. They are grouped in stacks. The membranes are called **grana**.

Inside the membranes are pigments. A pigment is a substance that absorbs, or takes in, light. The most important pigment in a chloroplast is chlorophyll (KLAWR uh fihl). **Chlorophyll** absorbs most colors of light, but it does not absorb green. This gives plants their green color.

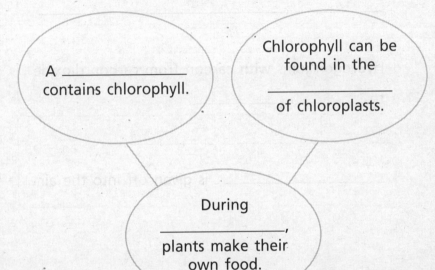

1. Fill in the blanks.
   During photosynthesis, plants turn

   _____ and _____

   into _____.

2. Complete the diagram.

   A _____ contains chlorophyll.

   Chlorophyll can be found in the _____ of chloroplasts.

   During _____, plants make their own food.

I Wonder . . . Chlorophyll reflects green light. What if chlorophyll absorbed all colors except blue? What would plants look like? Why would they look that way?

_____

_____

_____

33

3. Complete the diagram to tell about the process of photosynthesis.

Sunlight shines on _____.

↓

The energy from the sunlight is used to

_____.

↓

Hydrogen joins with carbon from carbon dioxide

to _____.

↓

_____ is given off into the air.

4. In what organelle does photosynthesis take place?

_____

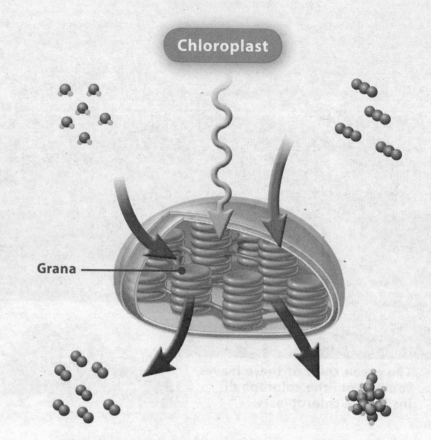

Chloroplast

Grana ——

Stacks of membranes called grana contain chlorophyll. Chlorophyll absorbs sunlight.

When light shines on chlorophyll, the energy is used to break up water molecules. Later, hydrogen joins with carbon from carbon dioxide to form sugars. Oxygen gas is put into the air.

The next time you see a tree or a plant, remember that almost all of it came from only water and carbon dioxide.

Plant Leaves

Plant leaves come in many different shapes and sizes. Leaves hold most of a plant's chloroplasts.

The broad, flat part of a leaf is called the blade. Leaves are made of different tissues. The outer layer is called the epidermis. The cells in this tissue have a waterproof coating. This keeps it from losing water.

Most of the cells that do photosynthesis lie just below the epidermis.

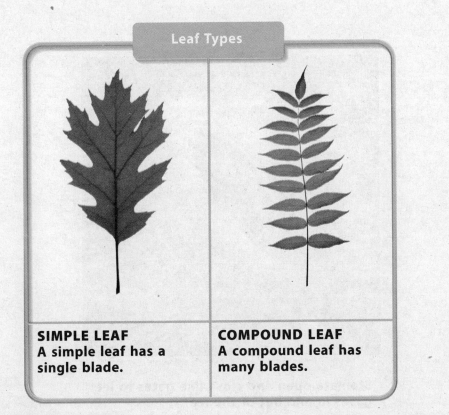

Leaf Types

SIMPLE LEAF
A simple leaf has a single blade.

COMPOUND LEAF
A compound leaf has many blades.

5. Fill in the blanks.

   a. The broad, flat part of a leaf is called the _____.

   b. A _____ leaf has a single blade.

   c. A _____ leaf has many blades.

   d. The outer layer of a leaf is called the _____.

6. In what part of the leaf are most of the cells that do photosynthesis?

   _____

7. What are stomata? Tell what stomata do.

_____

_____

_____

I Wonder . . . Can photosynthesis take place when the stomata are closed? What do you think?

_____

_____

_____

Small holes in the epidermis allow oxygen and carbon dioxide to enter or exit the leaf. They also allow water vapor to exit. These openings are called **stomata** (STOH mah tuh) and are all over the bottom of a leaf. Carbon dioxide enters the leaf through the stomata. Oxygen and water vapor exit there.

Stomata are open during the day for photosynthesis. At night, stomata close to keep water in.

Long, thin tubes running through leaves are called veins. Veins carry things in and out of the leaf. They connect the leaf's cells to the rest of the plant.

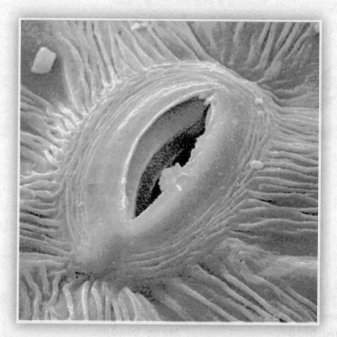

Stomata open and close like gates to let gases in and out of the leaf.

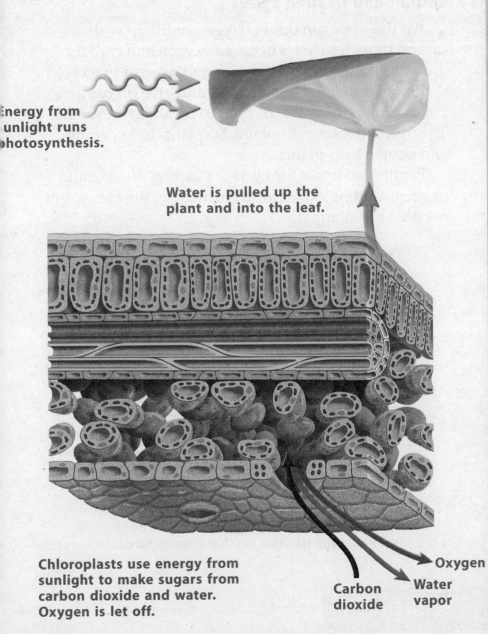

Energy from sunlight runs photosynthesis.

Water is pulled up the plant and into the leaf.

Chloroplasts use energy from sunlight to make sugars from carbon dioxide and water. Oxygen is let off.

Carbon dioxide

Oxygen

Water vapor

8. Use the following words and hints to add labels to the diagram of the leaf on this page. Read the hint. Then write the word on the diagram and draw an arrow from the word to the correct leaf part.

Leaf Part	Hint
Upper Epidermis	The epidermis is the "skin" of the leaf.
Lower Epidermis	The leaf has skin on both its top and its bottom.
Stomata	The stomata are openings in the leaf.
Chloroplasts	Chloroplasts are near the upper surface of the leaf so that sunlight can easily strike them.
Vein	The veins in a leaf are similar to the veins in your body in that they are tubes for carrying materials.

Summary Plants use energy from the Sun to make food through a process called photosynthesis. They combine carbon dioxide and water to make sugar, and they release oxygen in the process. In which organelle of the plant does photosynthesis occur?

_____

Sequence How do carbon and oxygen cycle through the atmosphere?

Animal releases _____ when it exhales.

_____ enters atmosphere.

_____ is taken in by plant.

Photosynthesis uses carbon from _____ to make sugars.

Plant releases _____ into the atmosphere.

Animal breathes in _____ from the atmosphere.

Animal uses the oxygen to break down sugars.

Carbon and Oxygen Cycles

Air does not run out of oxygen or fill up with carbon dioxide. This is because oxygen and carbon dioxide go through the air over and over, or in a cycle.

Plants take in carbon dioxide and give off oxygen. Plants and animals use oxygen to break down sugars. They give off carbon dioxide. So plants help people, and people help plants.

People can upset the cycles of carbon dioxide and oxygen. Cutting down forests can upset the cycles, but people keep doing it.

Carbon dioxide and oxygen cycle through plants, animals, and Earth's atmosphere.

SEQUENCE

How do carbon and oxygen cycle through the atmosphere?

How Do Plants Move Materials?

Plants have tissues and use energy to move water, minerals, and nutrients.

Limits to Growth

Most plants you can name are vascular plants. A **vascular plant** has special tissues that move things through it. Veins carry things in and out of leaves and through roots and stems. Veins are vascular tissues.

Have you ever seen moss growing on the side of a tree? Mosses are nonvascular plants. **Nonvascular plants** do not have parts that move sugar, water, and other things between plant parts. They also do not have true leaves, stems, or roots.

MOSSES AND LIVERWORTS
Nonvascular plants lack complex organs. Some of their leaf-like tissues are only one cell thick.

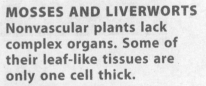

Moss

Liverwort

VOCABULARY

nonvascular plant a plant that lacks true leaves, stems, and roots *(noun)*

phloem a vascular tissue that conducts food that is made in the leaves to the rest of the plant *(noun)*

transpiration the evaporation of water through a plant's leaves *(noun)*

vascular plant a plant that has specialized structures for transporting food, water, and other materials between plant parts *(noun)*

xylem a vascular tissue that conducts water and minerals through a plant *(noun)*

VOCABULARY SKILL: Antonyms

The prefix *non-* is often used to form the antonym of a word, or its opposite. For example, the words *renewable* and *nonrenewable* are opposites. A vascular plant has specialized structures for moving materials within the plant. Use this definition and the information about *non-* to write a definition of a *nonvascular plant*.

_____

_____

 2.a. Students know that many living things have structures to transport materials.
2.e. Students know how materials are moved in a vascular plant.

39

1. Why are nonvascular plants so small?

_____

_____

2. Complete the diagram to tell how nonvascular plants affect the soil in which they grow.

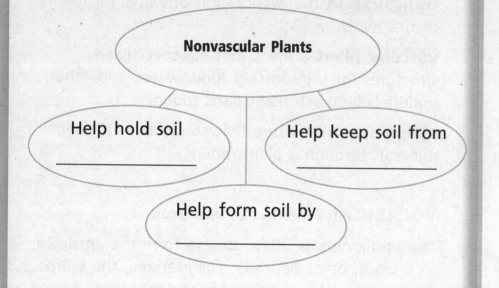

Nonvascular Plants

Help hold soil

_____

Help keep soil from

_____

Help form soil by

_____

Nonvascular plants are almost always small. This is because they do not have a way to move water to parts that are far away. Most of their cells must be close to something that has water, such as the ground or the side of a tree.

Nonvascular plants help hold soil in place and keep it from drying out. They also help form soil. Nonvascular plants such as moss break down the rocks that they grow on. These plants also give insects and other small animals food and a place to live.

Like this sponge, a cell will slowly take up water from the outside. The slow speed limits the size of the cell and of the organism.

TRUNKS
Growth rings mark each year's new xylem, or wood tissue. The darker parts show where growth slowed at the end of each season.

Vascular Plants

Vascular plants have roots, stems, and leaves. Roots keep a plant in the ground. They soak up water and minerals from the soil. Some roots store food for the plant as well.

The stem holds the plant up. It holds the plant's leaves up in the air so they can get sunlight. The stem is a way for water, minerals, and sugars to move between the roots and the leaves.

3. Vascular plants have parts for moving materials. Read each description. Tell whether it describes a root or a stem.

Plant Part	What It Does
_____	It keeps the plant in the ground.
_____	It holds up the plant.
_____	It soaks up water and minerals from the soil.
_____	It may store food.
_____	Is a way for materials to move between the leaves and roots.
_____	It holds up the leaves so they can get sunlight.

4. List two kinds of vascular tissue that can be found in roots, stems, and leaves.

a. _____

b. _____

5. Compare and contrast xylem and phloem.

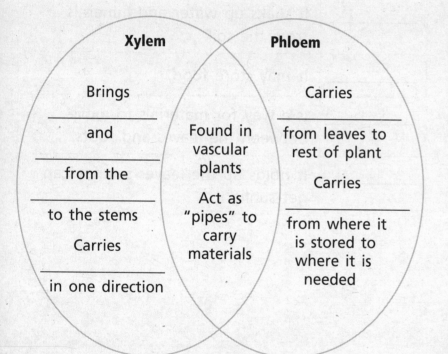

Xylem

Brings

_____

and

_____

from the

_____

to the stems

Carries

_____

in one direction

Found in vascular plants

Act as "pipes" to carry materials

Phloem

Carries

_____

from leaves to rest of plant

Carries

_____

from where it is stored to where it is needed

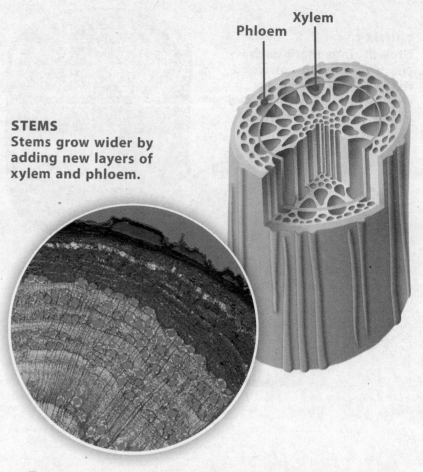

Phloem   Xylem

STEMS
Stems grow wider by adding new layers of xylem and phloem.

Roots, stems, and leaves have two kinds of vascular tissues: xylem and phloem. **Xylem** (ZY luhm) brings water and minerals from the roots to the stem and the leaves. It carries water in one direction.

Phloem (FLOH ehm) brings sugar that is made in the leaves down to the rest of the plant. The food is either used or stored. Phloem also can bring sugar up from where it is stored to where it is needed.

The Upward Flow of Water

Water and minerals move up plants because of root pressure, cohesion, and transpiration.

Root Pressure Water enters roots because roots are saltier than the soil. The outer walls of roots have cells that keep water from leaking back out. Pressure is a force that builds and pushes the water up.

TRANSPIRATION
Evaporation from the leaves creates a pull that draws water up through the stem.

GRAVITY
Sugar from photosynthesis is pulled down to nourish the plant.

COHESION
Water and minerals cling to each other and to the xylem walls. This forms a column that rises up the stem.

ROOT PRESSURE
Root pressure pushes water and minerals up.

6. Why does water in the soil enter a plant's roots?

_____

_____

7. What force causes water drops to cling to one another?

_____

8. What pulls water and minerals up the xylem of a plant?

_____

9. Use the captions on this page to help you complete the diagram.

Water and minerals move up plants because of

_____   _____

_____

10. Put a check next to each statement that is true about movement of water and nutrients through a vascular plant. Put an X by each statement that is false.

_____ Root pressure alone is strong enough to push water through a plant.

_____ Water molecules cling to one another as a result of a force called cohesion.

_____ Adhesion pulls water down.

_____ Transpiration sends water to the highest parts of a plant.

11. What are the largest vascular plants?

_____

Transpiration draws water up these tall redwood trees. The record-holder is 112 meters high!

Cohesion Root pressure alone does not push much water through the plant. Water is pulled up, too.

Water drops stick to each other because of a force called cohesion. They stick to other things, too. This force is called adhesion. Adhesion forces water to climb up tubes of xylem tissue.

Transpiration More pull is needed to move water to the tops of tall plants. That pull comes from transpiration. **Transpiration** is the evaporation of water through a plant's leaves. Transpiration creates a pulling force that draws water to the highest parts of a tree or plant.

How Wide? How Tall?

Vascular plants can be very small or they can be very large. The largest vascular plants are trees.

A tree's size depends on the things around it. A tree grows best when it gets all of the nutrients, water, and sunlight it needs. It will not grow as tall if it is too wet or too dry. It will not grow as tall if it is too hot, cold, or windy.

The most important thing that decides the height of a tree is its vascular system. New stems and leaves will only grow if they have enough water and minerals.

Strong winds helped shape this tree on the California coast.

COMPARE AND CONTRAST

Compare the different forces that move water up a plant.

Summary Plants have specialized tissues and use natural forces to transport water, minerals, and nutrients. List three factors that affect how tall a tree will grow.

_____

_____

_____

_____

Compare and Contrast Compare the different forces that move materials up a plant.

Description of Force	Name of Force
Evaporation from leaves creates a pulling force.	_____
Water and minerals clinging to one another form a column that rises up the stem.	_____
Pressure from below pushes water and minerals upward.	_____

Group two or more words in this glossary together. Then tell why they go together.

chlorophyll (KLAWR uh fihl) the pigment in a chloroplast that absorbs light

clorofila en un cloroplasto, pigmento que absorbe la luz

chloroplast (KLAWR uh PLAST) an organelle in plant cells in which photosynthesis takes place

cloroplasto orgánulo en las células de las plantas en el que tiene lugar la fotosíntesis

grana stacks of membranes inside a chloroplast that contain chlorophyll

grana conjunto de membranas dentro de un cloroplasto que contienen clorofila

nonvascular plant a plant that lacks true leaves, stems, and roots

planta no vascular planta que carece de hojas, tallo y raíces

phloem (FLOH ehm) a vascular tissue that conducts food that is made in the leaves to the rest of the plant

floema tejido vascular que transporta hacia el resto de la planta el alimento producido en las hojas

photosynthesis (foh toh SIHN thih sihs) the process by which plants transform energy from sunlight into chemical energy

fotosíntesis proceso mediante el cual las plantas transfoman energía de la luz solar en energía química

Glossary

stomata (STOH mah tuh) small openings in the bottom of a leaf through which gases move

estomas pequeñas aperturas en la parte inferior de una hoja a través de las cuales fluyen los gases

transpiration the evaporation of water through a plant's leaves

transpiración evaporación del agua a través de las hojas de una planta

vascular plant a plant that has specialized structures for transporting food, water, and other materials between plant parts

planta vascular planta que tiene estructuras especializadas para transportar alimentos, agua y otros materiales a las diversas partes de la planta

xylem (ZY luhm) a vascular tissue that conducts water and minerals through a plant

xilema tejido vascular que conduce agua y minerales a través de la planta

 Visit www.eduplace.com to play puzzles and word games.

Circle the word in this glossary that is the same in both English and Spanish.

KWL

WHAT DID YOU LEARN?

Vocabulary

❶ (Circle) the correct answer on the page.

Comprehension

❷ _____

_____

_____

_____

❸ _____

_____

❹ _____

_____

_____

_____

Critical Thinking

❺ _____

_____

_____

_____

Think About What You Have Read

Vocabulary

❶ Photosynthesis takes place in an organelle called a/an _____.

A) chlorophyll

B) chloroplast

C) phloem

D) stomata

Comprehension

❷ How are the tissues of a leaf arranged?

❸ What do the two types of vascular tissues conduct?

❹ How does transpiration allow a plant to grow tall?

Critical Thinking

❺ What would you say to someone who said that people don't need plants? Include at least three reasons in your answer.

Human Body Systems

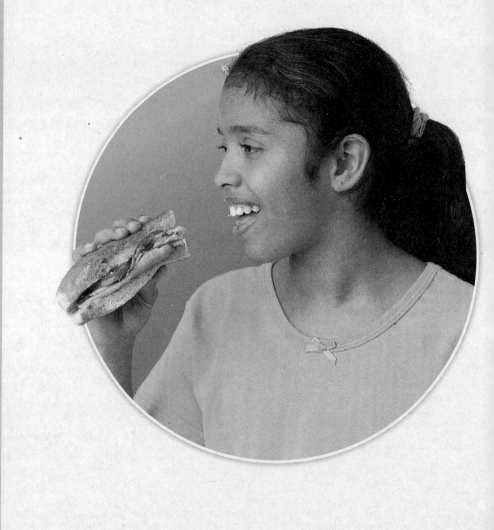

KWL

WHAT DO YOU KNOW?

List one fact about each of these human body systems:

a. Respiratory system _____

_____

_____

b. Circulatory system _____

_____

_____

c. Digestive system _____

_____

_____

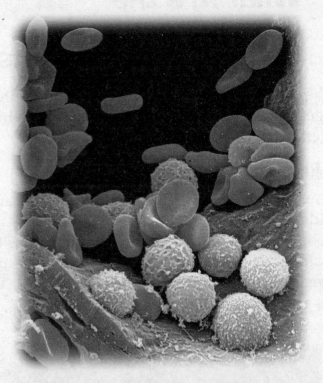

Contents

KWL

WHAT DO YOU WANT TO KNOW?

Skim the pictures and headings in this chapter. List one thing you want to find out about each of these body systems:

a. Respiratory system _____
_____
_____

b. Circulatory system _____
_____
_____

c. Digestive system _____
_____
_____

1

What Are the Respiratory and Circulatory Systems?

VOCABULARY

artery a blood vessel that carries blood away from the heart *(noun)*

capillary a very thin vessel in which gases, nutrients, and wastes pass to and from the body cells *(noun)*

circulatory system a system that works to bring oxygen and nutrients to body cells and takes away carbon dioxide and wastes *(noun)*

heart a muscular organ at the center of the circulatory system that pumps blood through a network of blood vessels *(noun)*

respiratory system a system of organs that exchange gases with the environment *(noun)*

vein a blood vessel that carries blood back to the heart *(noun)*

VOCABLARY SKILL: Word Origins

Circulatory comes from the Latin word *circulus,* which means "circle." How does the meaning of *circulus* relate to the circulatory system?

_____

_____

The respiratory system brings oxygen into the body and gets rid of wastes. The circulatory system brings oxygen to the cells and carries off wastes.

The Respiratory System

Your body takes in oxygen and gets rid of carbon dioxide with every breath.

People and animals have a system of organs that work together—the respiratory system. The **respiratory system** is what helps meet our need to breathe. The lungs are the organs that help you breathe.

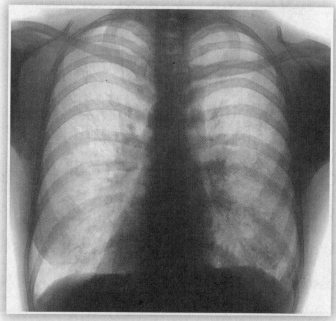

Your lungs take in gases from the air with each breath you take.

2.a. Students know that many living things have structures to transport materials.
2.b. Students know how blood circulates in the body and how gases are exchanged.

You breathe in and air moves from your nose to a tube called the trachea. The trachea leads to two big tubes called bronchial tubes. These tubes divide into smaller and smaller tubes. The smallest tubes lead to tiny air sacs called alveoli.

The lungs hold millions of alveoli. Next to all of the alveoli is a capillary, a thin tube that holds blood. The exchange of oxygen and carbon dioxide takes place between a capillary and one of the alveoli. You exhale carbon dioxide.

Respiratory System

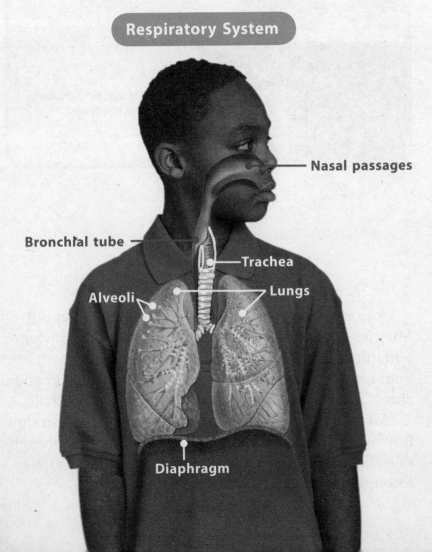

— Nasal passages

Bronchial tube —

—Trachea

Alveoli

—Lungs

Diaphragm

1. Complete the diagram to show how air moves from your nose into the smallest sacs of your lungs.

> Air moves from your nose to a tube called the
> _____.

> The _____ leads to two big tubes
> called _____.

> These tubes divide into _____ tubes.

> The smallest tubes lead to tiny air sacs called
> _____.

2. Where does the exchange of oxygen and carbon dioxide take place?

   _____

3. What gas do you exhale?

   _____

4. Complete the diagram to tell what happens to make more space in your chest when you breathe in air.

Muscles attached to your ribs pull _____.

↓

Your diaphragm pulls _____.

I Wonder . . . Why do humans and other animals need a respiratory system? What do you think?

_____

_____

_____

_____

_____

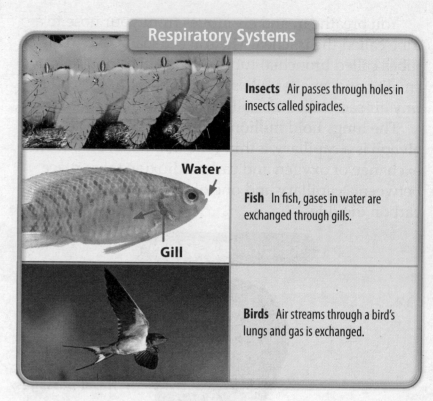

Respiratory Systems

Insects Air passes through holes in insects called spiracles.

Water

Fish In fish, gases in water are exchanged through gills.

Gill

Birds Air streams through a bird's lungs and gas is exchanged.

Your chest changes size as you breathe in and out. Muscles attached to the ribs tighten and pull up when you inhale. The diaphragm, a muscle at the bottom of your chest, pulls down. This makes more space in your chest. The opposite action happens when you exhale.

All animals need oxygen. Insects take in air through tiny holes called spiracles. Fish take in oxygen through gills. Birds in flight need a lot of oxygen. Gases move through a bird's body in one direction only.

The Circulatory System

The **circulatory system** brings oxygen and nutrients to all the cells of your body. Nutrients are things that all plants and animals need to live. The circulatory system takes carbon dioxide and wastes away from the cells. The gases, nutrients, and wastes all travel in blood.

The circulatory system connects every cell in your body. At the center of the circulatory system is a muscular organ called the **heart**. The heart pumps blood through blood vessels.

Circulatory System

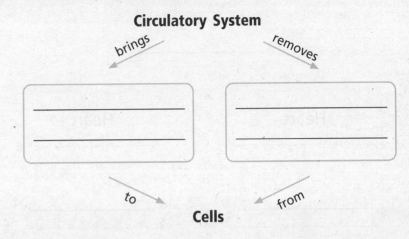

HEART
The heart is a pump about the size of your fist.

5. Complete the diagram to tell what the circulatory system does.

Circulatory System

brings   removes

_____   _____

_____   _____

to   from

Cells

6. What organ is the main part of the circulatory system? Circle that organ in the picture.

_____

55

7. Complete the diagram to show how blood moves through the circulatory system.

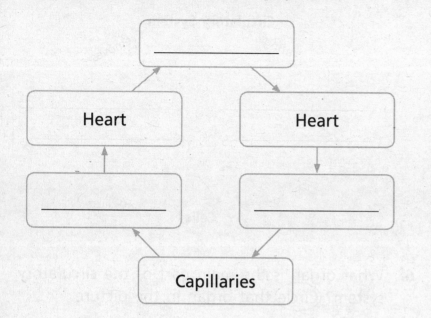

Heart

Heart

Capillaries

8. List four materials that are passed between capillaries and body cells.

a. _____

b. _____

c. _____

d. _____

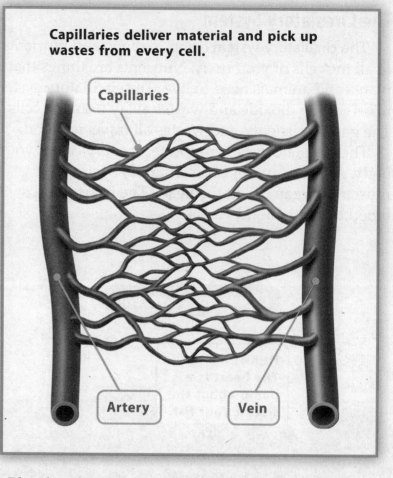

Capillaries deliver material and pick up wastes from every cell.

Capillaries

Artery

Vein

Blood picks up oxygen in the lungs. Then it goes to the heart. Blood then passes through arteries to all other parts of the body. An **artery** is a blood vessel that carries blood away from the heart.

Arteries branch into tiny, thin vessels called **capillaries**. Gases, sugars, minerals, and wastes pass between capillaries and body cells.

Capillaries lead to veins. A **vein** is a blood vessel that carries blood back to the heart. The blood in veins contains mostly carbon dioxide. The blood is pumped to the lungs once again.

Blood contains red blood cells, white blood cells, platelets, and other parts. Red blood cells are disc shaped. These cells contain hemoglobin. Hemoglobin carries oxygen, carbon dioxide, and the mineral iron. Hemoglobin gives blood its red color.

White blood cells are larger cells that help the body fight disease or illness. Blood also contains platelets.

Platelets are small pieces of cells. Platelets help the blood clump together in a clot. This helps to stop bleeding and heal cuts.

Blood cells and platelets are carried in plasma, the liquid part of blood. Plasma also carries sugars and water to the cells. It carries wastes to the kidneys.

9. a. Blood gets its red color from _____.

   b. This material carries _____, _____, and _____.

10. Complete the chart to tell about the parts of blood.

Blood Part	Description
_____	Helps the body fight disease
_____	Contains hemoglobin
_____	Helps stop bleeding
_____	The liquid part of blood

11. List the four chambers of the human heart.

a. _____

b. _____

c. _____

d. _____

12. Complete the sentences to tell about the human heart.

a. The _____ pump blood to the body.

b. Each atrium receives blood from the

_____.

13. On the picture of the heart, (circle) the four veins that carry blood to the heart from the lungs.

The Heart

The human heart is divided into four chambers, or sections. The two upper chambers are called the left atrium and right atrium. They bring in blood from the veins. The two lower chambers are called the ventricles. The ventricles pump blood to the body.

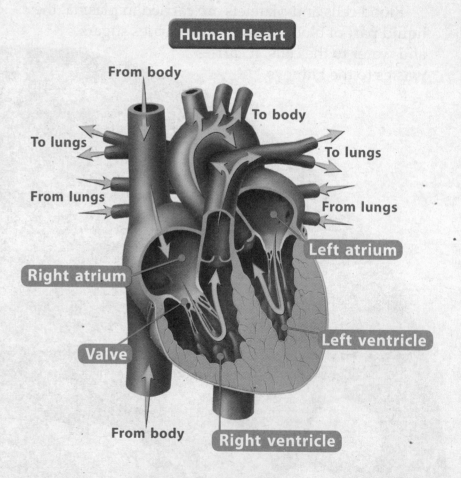

Human Heart

From body

To body

To lungs

To lungs

From lungs

From lungs

Left atrium

Right atrium

Valve

Left ventricle

From body

Right ventricle

Most animals have some kind of heart and circulatory system. A frog's heart has three chambers. A fish heart has only two chambers. An earthworm has five hearts, each with one chamber.

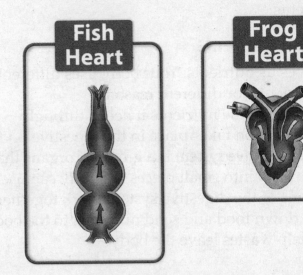

Fish Heart

Frog Heart

Summary The respiratory system brings oxygen into the body and removes wastes. The circulatory system carries oxygen to the cells and carries away wastes.

What organ is at the center of the circulatory system?

_____

Compare and Contrast Compare how a fish and a human breathe.

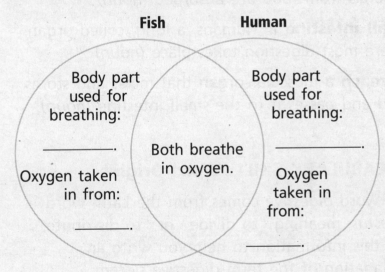

Fish   Human

Body part used for breathing:

_____.

Oxygen taken in from:

_____.

Both breathe in oxygen.

Body part used for breathing:

_____.

Oxygen taken in from:

_____.

VOCABULARY

digestive system an organ system that breaks down food to release nutrients *(noun)*

esophagus a muscular tube that pushes food toward the stomach *(noun)*

large intestine the organ into which food and other substances pass and where water and minerals from food are absorbed *(noun)*

small intestine in humans, a long, coiled organ where most digestion takes place *(noun)*

stomach a muscular organ that mixes and stores food and passes it to the small intestine *(noun)*

VOCABULARY SKILL: Word Origins

The word *digestive* comes from the Latin word *digestus*, meaning "to divide" or "to distribute." Use this information to help you write an explanation of the term *digestive system*.

_____

_____

2

What Is the Digestive System?

Living things need nutrients from food. The digestive system breaks down food to release these nutrients.

Energy from Nutrients

Food gives us nutrients. Your body uses different kinds of nutrients for different reasons.

Your body gets the nutrients it needs through digestion. Digestion takes place in the digestive system. The **digestive system** is a group of organs that break down food into small pieces the body can use.

The organs of the digestive system work together. They break down food and send nutrients to the body. They also help wastes leave the body.

A long digestive system with many chambers helps a horse digest grass.

2.c. Students know how food is digested and what the organs of the digestive system do.

You should eat many different foods to stay healthy. Healthy foods give you the nutrients your body needs. Drinking lots of water also helps keep you healthy. The digestive system needs water to work best.

It's important to eat right every day and avoid eating too many fats and sweets. Your body can store some nutrients, but vitamins and minerals cannot be stored. Your body needs a steady supply of these nutrients to stay healthy.

Nutrients

Carbohydrates	Proteins	Vitamins and Minerals	Fats
Carbohydrates are the main source of energy for the body.	Proteins are used to replace, repair, and grow new cells and tissue.	Vitamins and minerals help your body in many ways.	Fats are a source of energy and keep your skin healthy. They also help the body use vitamins and cushion body organs.
Sources • whole-grain bread • pasta • rice and other grains • potatoes	Sources • fish • beef • chicken • beans • eggs • cheese	Sources • fruits • vegetables • fortified milk	Sources • butter • oil • salad dressing • ice cream

1. Complete the outline about the digestive system.

   I. You must take in food.

      A. Food provides the body with _____.

      B. The body uses different kinds of _____ for different purposes.

   II. Your body gets the nutrients it needs from food in a process called _____.

      A. The _____ _____ is a group of organs that breaks down food.

      B. The food is broken down into _____ _____ that your body can use.

   III. Healthy foods provide your body with _____.

      A. The digestive system needs _____ to work best.

      B. You should avoid eating too many _____ and _____.

      C. Your body needs a steady supply of _____ and _____ to stay healthy.

2. Complete the diagram to show how enzymes work in the digestive system.

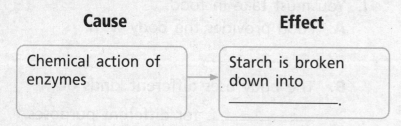

Cause		Effect
Chemical action of enzymes	→	Starter is broken down into _____.

3. Saliva is a watery liquid that comes from the salivary glands. (Circle) these glands in the photo.

I Wonder . . . What would happen to a person's digestive process if fewer enzymes were produced?

_____

_____

_____

_____

Stages of Digestion

Digestion begins in the mouth. Chewing grinds food into smaller pieces. Your tongue mixes the food with saliva.

Saliva is the watery liquid in the mouth. It breaks down food. Saliva contains chemicals called enzymes. Enzymes break down the starch in foods such as bread and potatoes. Starches break down into sugars.

Chewed food moves from the mouth into the esophagus when you swallow. The **esophagus** (uh SAHF uh gihs) is a muscular tube that pushes food toward the stomach.

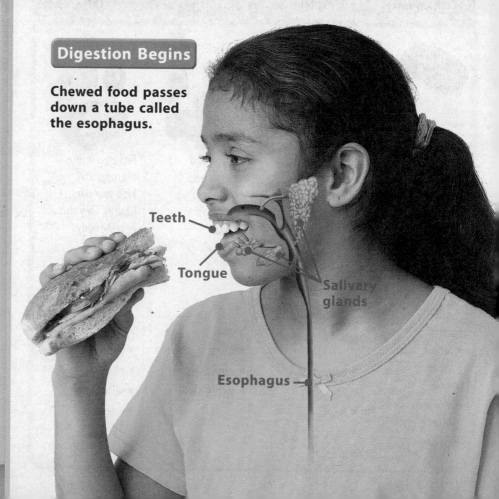

Digestion Begins

Chewed food passes down a tube called the esophagus.

Teeth

Tongue

Salivary glands

Esophagus

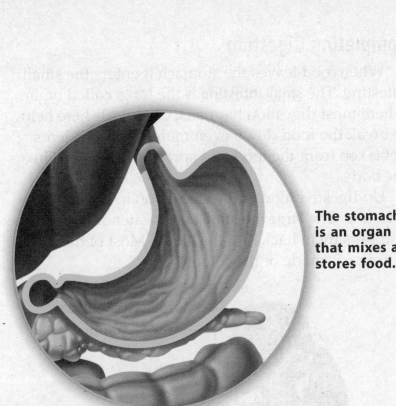

The stomach is an organ that mixes and stores food.

The **stomach** is a muscular organ that mixes and stores food and turns it into a soupy mix. Cells lining the stomach release fluids that help to break down food.

The stomach squeezes the food and mixes it with digestive fluids. The fluids contain enzymes and an acid. This acid is a strong chemical that breaks down food.

After food has been in your stomach for one to three hours, it leaves your stomach. The food is on its way to becoming nutrients your cells can use.

4. Complete this diagram to show what happens when food moves from your mouth to your stomach.

_____ grinds food into smaller pieces.

Your tongue mixes _____ with the food.

Food moves from your mouth to your _____ when you swallow.

Food travels to a muscular organ called the _____.

Cells lining this organ release digestive _____ that help break down the food.

The food mixes with digestive fluids in the _____.

After one to three hours, the food is close to being nutrients that your _____ can use.

Summary To function properly, living things need nutrients found in foods. The digestive system breaks down food to release these nutrients.

In what part of the digestive system does most digestion occur?

_____

In what part of the digestive system are water and minerals taken from the food?

_____

Main Idea and Details What is one role of the stomach?

Main idea: The stomach mixes the food with digestive fluids.

Detail: Cells lining the stomach release fluids that help

_____.

Detail: Stomach fluids contain

_____ and

an _____.

64

Completing Digestion

When food leaves the stomach it enters the small intestine. The **small intestine** is the long, coiled organ where most digestion happens. Chemicals here help to break the food down even more. Then nutrients get taken from the food and spread to every cell in the body.

Undigested food and waste go on to the large intestine. The **large intestine** takes water and minerals and puts them back into the blood. Most of the large intestine is made of the colon.

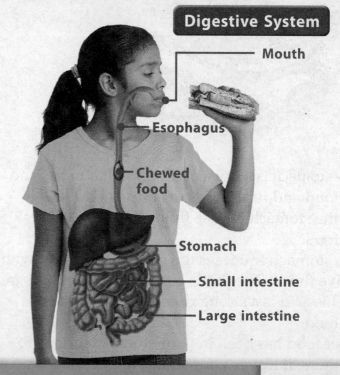

Digestive System

- Mouth
- Esophagus
- Chewed food
- Stomach
- Small intestine
- Large intestine

MAIN IDEA AND DETAILS

What is one role of the stomach?

What Is the Excretory System?

All living things make wastes. The excretory system removes wastes and helps keep the body's water balanced.

The Excretory System

A huge number of reactions take place in your body. These reactions break down food into smaller pieces, bring oxygen to red blood cells, and capture the energy from food.

These reactions cause the body to produce a lot of waste. A waste is any material that the body cannot use. The job of the **excretory system** is to remove wastes and to keep the body's water balanced.

Excretory System

Filtered blood returns to the body

Body cells create wastes.

The kidneys filter wastes.

Wastes are removed from the body.

The liver converts wastes into urea.

Blood carries wastes to liver.

Blood carries urea to kidneys.

VOCABULARY

bladder a muscular bag that holds urine *(noun)*

excretory system an organ system that removes wastes and maintains water balance *(noun)*

kidney a bean-shaped organ that filters wastes from the blood *(noun)*

VOCABULARY SKILL: Word Content

The word *excretory* comes from the Latin word *excretus*, which means "to sift out." When you sift something like soil, you remove the unwanted materials, such as rocks. What does the excretory system do?

_____

_____

2.d. Students know what kidneys do.

65

1. Complete the chart to tell about the excretory system.

Blood carries wastes that contain _____, a gas, to the _____.

↓

The liver converts _____ to _____.

↓

Blood carries the _____ to the kidneys.

↓

The _____ take wastes from the blood.

↓

The liquid remaining after the blood is cleaned is called _____.

↓

Urine leaves the kidney and flows down the _____.

↓

Urine is stored in the _____.

Wastes from the digestive tract that the body does not need for nutrients becomes solid waste. The blood moves other wastes out of the body. Blood carries wastes that contain nitrogen, a gas. The liver changes nitrogen into a compound called urea.

Blood then carries the urea to the kidneys. Filtering urea from the blood is the main job of the kidneys. The **kidneys** are bean-shaped organs that are near the middle of the back. People have two kidneys. Kidneys take waste from blood. The liquid that remains after the blood is cleaned is called urine.

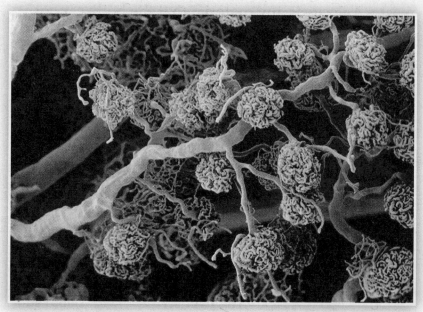

Inside your kidneys, wastes filter out of blood to form urine.

Excretory System

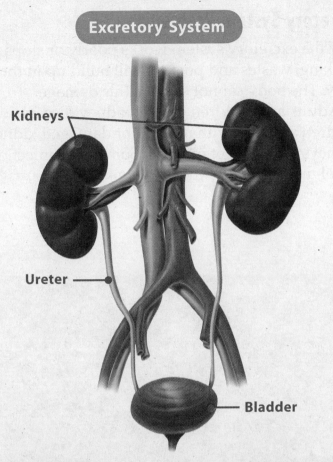

The excretory system gets rid of the body's waste. Urine is stored in the bladder before the body gets rid of it.

When urine leaves the kidneys, it flows down tubes called ureters. These tubes lead to the bladder. The **bladder** is a muscular bag that holds urine. Sensors signal the brain when the bladder needs to be emptied.

Kidneys also help the body keep the right amount of water. The kidneys need to be well protected. They are surrounded by a layer of fat. They are also kept away from the part of the body that holds the organs of the digestive system.

2. Complete the table. Write the name of the body part next to its description.

Description	Body Parts
Carries wastes to the kidneys	_____
Bean-shaped organs near the middle of the back	_____
A muscular bag that holds urine	_____
Filters urea from the blood	_____
Tubes that lead to the bladder	_____
Changes nitrogen into a compound called urea	_____

67

3. Complete the diagram.

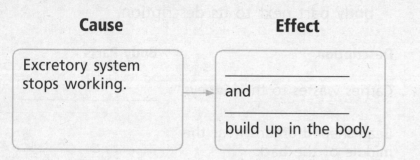

Cause		Effect
Excretory system stops working.	→	_____ and _____ build up in the body.

4. List three problems that can occur to kidneys.

a. _____

b. _____

c. _____

Excretory System Problems

If the excretory system works poorly or stops working, wastes and poisons will build up in the body. The body cannot survive this damage.

Adults and children can get kidney disease. Some children are born with missing or damaged kidneys. Kidneys can also get infected. Sometimes infections travel up the urinary tubes to the kidneys.

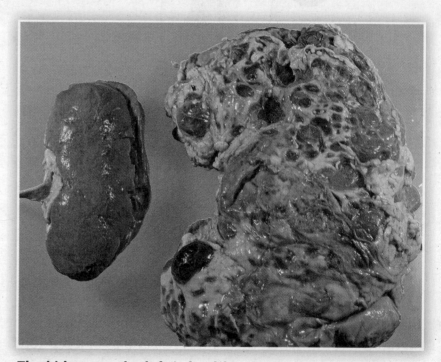

The kidney on the left is healthy. Compare it with the diseased kidney on the right.

People sometimes get kidney stones. Kidney stones are groups of salts or minerals. Large kidney stones can be very painful.

Kidneys can be damaged from an injury, such as a sharp blow to the lower back. A car accident or bad fall could also hurt the kidneys.

You can keep your kidneys healthy by drinking lots of water and eating healthy food. Following safety rules during exercise also helps prevent injuries.

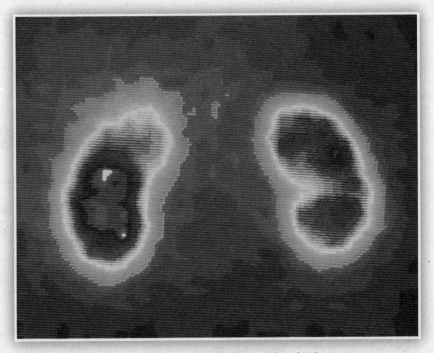

The special photo shows blood flow. The kidney on the left has normal blood flow. The kidney on the right has poor blood flow.

5. List three ways to keep your kidneys healthy.

a. _____

b. _____

c. _____

6. Look at the photo on this page. Which color probably represents blood flow?

_____

69

7. Complete the diagram to tell when dialysis is needed.

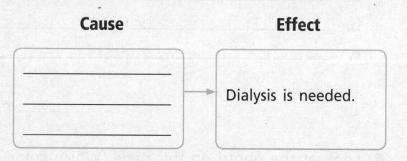

Cause | Effect
_____
_____ → Dialysis is needed.
_____

8. Number the steps to show the order that describes dialysis.

_____ Wastes are filtered from blood in a machine.

_____ Filtered blood is returned to the body.

_____ Blood containing wastes is removed from the body.

Dialysis

Dialysis is needed when kidneys stop working. Dialysis is a way to clean the blood.

There are two kinds of dialysis. In one method, a machine cleans waste and extra fluid from the blood. The machine returns the clean blood back to the patient's body.

Another kind of dialysis uses the patient's body as the blood cleaner. A drug helps turn tissues in the body into a simple blood cleaner. A machine pumps in the drug and drains out the wastes.

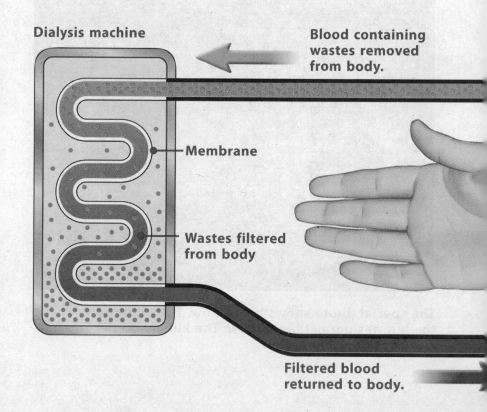

Dialysis machine

Blood containing wastes removed from body.

Membrane

Wastes filtered from body

Filtered blood returned to body.

A long-lasting treatment for a sick kidney is to transplant a new kidney. A doctor cuts out the damaged kidney and puts a new, healthy kidney into the patient's body. People only need one working kidney to stay healthy.

Kidney transplants do not always work. Sometimes the body tries to reject, or not work with, organs and tissues that are not its own. It helps if the new kidney is from a close relative of the patient.

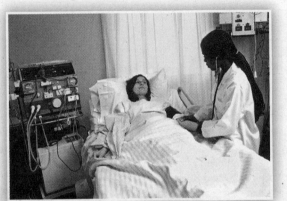

Dialysis has saved many lives.

9. List three treatments that can be used if the kidneys stop working.

a. _____

_____

b. _____

_____

c. _____

_____

10. Complete the diagram to show how dialysis and drug therapy for kidney failure are similar and different.

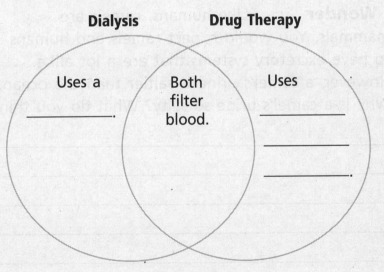

Dialysis   Drug Therapy

Uses a _____.

Both filter blood.

Uses _____

_____

_____.

11. Write the name of the living thing next to the description of its waste removal system.

Living Thing	Waste Removal System
_____	Wastes pass directly to the outside through animal's wet skin
_____	Change nitrogen wastes to solid uric acid
_____	Make urea, which flushes out of body with water
_____	Store wastes in a vacuole

I Wonder . . . Like humans, camels are mammals. You would expect camels and humans to have excretory systems that are a lot alike. However, a camel's urine is saltier than the ocean. Why is a camel's urine so salty? What do you think?

_____

_____

_____

_____

Waste Removal in Other Organisms

All living things make wastes. There are many different ways to get rid of them.

In a small organism, water and gas wastes go directly out of the body. The wet skin of an earthworm takes in oxygen and releases waste.

Snakes and lizards change nitrogen waste to uric acid. Uric acid is a solid compound. It can be removed with very little water. This helps snakes and lizards live in dry places.

A camel's kidneys remove waste without losing a lot of water.

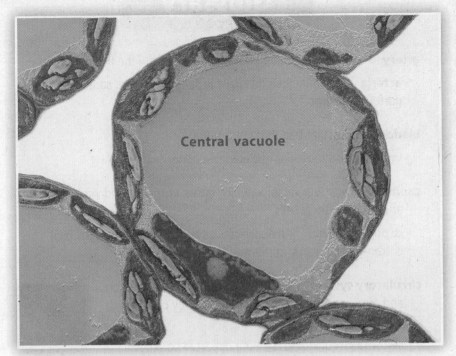

Central vacuole

Plant vacuoles can store cell waste products.

All mammals make urea, which is flushed out of the body with water. The kidneys of some desert animals do this very well. A camel has such powerful kidneys that its urine can be saltier than sea water.

Plants also make wastes. Plant cells keep wastes in a vacuole. The vacuole is a large sac in the middle of the cell. Plants may also keep wastes in parts it does not want anymore, such as the leaves a tree drops in autumn.

PROBLEM/SOLUTION

What are some treatments that can be used when kidneys stop working?

Summary   All living things produce wastes. In humans, the excretory system removes wastes and helps maintain water levels in the body.

List three parts of the human excretory system.

a. _____

b. _____

c. _____

Problem/Solution   What are some treatments that can be used when kidneys stop working?

Problem	Solution
Kidneys stop working.	1. _____ 2. _____ 3. _____

Fill in the web with vocabulary words related to the word in the center of the web.

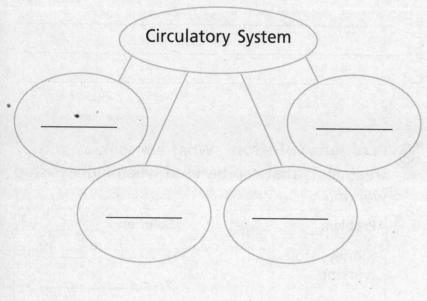

Circulatory System

artery a blood vessel that carries blood away from the heart

arteria vaso sanguíneo que lleva la sangre desde el corazón a otras partes del cuerpo

bladder a muscular bag that holds urine

vejiga bolsa muscular que contiene orina

capillary a very thin vessel in which gases, nutrients, and wastes pass to and from the body cells

capilar vaso muy fino de las células del cuerpo a través del cual entran y salen gases, nutrientes y desechos

circulatory system a system that works to bring oxygen and nutrients to body cells and takes away carbon dioxide and wastes

sistema circulatorio sistema que sirve para llevar oxígeno y nutrientes a las células del cuerpo y expulsar de ellas dióxido de carbono y desechos

digestive system an organ system that breaks down food to release nutrients

sistema digestivo sistema que separa los alimentos para liberar los nutrientes

esophagus (uh SAHF uh gihs) a muscular tube that pushes food toward the stomach

esófago tubo muscular que empuja los alimentos hacia el estómago

excretory system an organ system that removes wastes and maintains water balance

sistema excretorio sistema de órganos que elimina los desechos y mantiene el equilibrio del agua

Glossary

heart a muscular organ at the center of the circulatory system that pumps blood through a network of blood vessels

corazón órgano muscular en el centro del sistema circulatorio, que bombea sangre a través de una red de vasos sanguíneos

kidney a bean-shaped organ that filters wastes from the blood

riñón órgano con forma de frijol que filtra desechos procedentes de la sangre

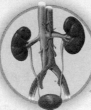

large intestine the organ into which food and other substances pass and where water and minerals from food are absorbed

intestino grueso órgano a través del cual pasan alimentos y otras sustancias y donde se absorbe agua y minerales de los alimentos

respiratory system a system of organs that exchange gases with the environment

sistema respiratorio sistema de órganos que intercambia gases con el ambiente

small intestine in humans, a long, coiled organ where most digestion takes place

intestino delgado en los humanos, órgano largo y enrollado donde tiene lugar la mayor parte de la digestión

stomach a muscular organ that mixes and stores food and passes it to the small intestine

estómago órgano muscular que mezcla y almacena alimento y lo pasa al intestino delgado

vein a blood vessel that carries blood back to the heart

vena vaso sanguíneo que transporta sangre de vuelta al corazón

 Visit www.eduplace.com to play puzzles and word games.

Find the English words that are like these Spanish words. List these words in the chart.

English	Spanish
	artería
	vena

Chapter Review

K W L

WHAT DID YOU LEARN?

Vocabulary

❶ (Circle) the correct answer on the page.

Comprehension

❷ _____
_____
_____

❸ _____
_____
_____

❹ _____
_____
_____

Critical Thinking

❺ _____
_____
_____

Think About What You Have Read

Vocabulary

❶ In the lungs, gas exchange occurs in tiny air sacs called _____.

   A) alveoli

   B) trachea

   C) bronchi

   D) villi

Comprehension

❷ Describe and compare the different chambers of the human heart.

❸ What does the digestive system do?

❹ Why do living things use different ways of removing wastes?

Critical Thinking

❺ Could the excretory system work without a healthy circulatory system? Explain.

KWL

WHAT DO YOU KNOW?

List one fact about each of these topics:

a. Where Earth's water can be found _____

_____

_____

b. How communities get water _____

_____

_____

c. How to use fresh water wisely _____

_____

_____

Water Resources

Contents

KWL

WHAT DO YOU WANT TO KNOW?
Skim the pictures and headings. List one thing you want to find out about each of these topics:

a. Earth's water resources _____

_____

_____

b. Where communities get their water _____

_____

_____

c. Using fresh water wisely _____

_____

VOCABULARY

desalination the removal of salt from salt water to make fresh water *(noun)*

groundwater water that collects in spaces and cracks in rocks and soil underground *(noun)*

runoff rainwater that flows over land without sinking into the soil *(noun)*

VOCABULARY SKILL: Compound Words

Groundwater is a compound word that refers to water found below the ground. What other compound words do you know that end with the word *water*?

_____

_____

3.a. Students know that most of Earth's water is salty and is found in oceans. Oceans cover most of Earth's surface.
3.d. Students know that fresh water is a limited resource.

80

1 Where Is Earth's Water?

Most of Earth's water is salt water in the oceans.

A Watery Planet

Earth is the only planet that is mostly covered by water. Almost all of Earth's water has salt in it. Salt water is in the oceans and seas.

Water is also found below and above the surface of Earth. There is some water in the rocks and soil. There is water in the air in the form of a gas. This gas is called water vapor.

No living thing on Earth can live without water.

Earth is sometimes called the "Big Blue Marble" because of how it looks from space.

Oceans and Seas

Almost three quarters of Earth's surface is covered by oceans and seas. Ocean water is salt water. It is not safe to drink.

The salt in ocean water comes from **runoff**, or rainwater that flows over the land without sinking into the soil. Water mixes with salts and minerals in soil and rock as it moves over the land. These salts and minerals are carried into rivers.

Rivers empty into oceans and seas, bringing the salts and minerals with them. This makes the ocean water salty.

Oceans cover about 70 percent of Earth's surface. Ocean water is too salty for humans to drink.

1. Complete the diagram to explain why ocean water is salty.

Rainwater flows as _____ over the land.

↓

The water mixes with _____ and _____ from the _____ and _____.

↓

These _____ and _____ are carried into _____.

↓

The _____ empty into _____ and _____, making them salty.

2. Complete the graph to show the percentage of Earth's surface that is salt water, land, and fresh water.

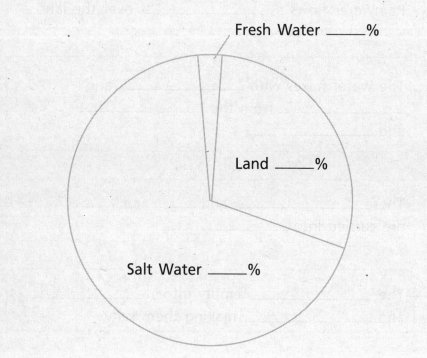

Fresh Water _____%

Land _____%

Salt Water _____%

3. Most of Earth's fresh water is "locked away" in _____ and _____.

Fresh Water on Earth

Many daily activities require fresh water. For some people, fresh water is not always close at hand.

Only three percent of Earth's water supply is fresh water. Humans and other living things need fresh water to survive. This is why fresh water is an important and valuable resource.

Two-thirds of the available fresh water is "locked away" in glaciers and polar ice caps. That leaves less than one percent of Earth's total water supply as fresh water that people can use to drink, cook, and grow food.

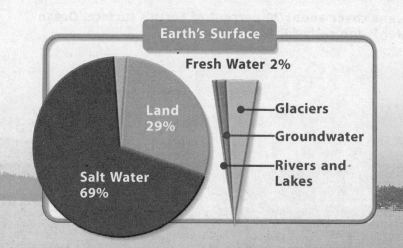

Earth's Surface

Fresh Water 2%

Land 29%

Glaciers

Groundwater

Rivers and Lakes

Salt Water 69%

Most of Earth's fresh water is frozen in glaciers and polar ice caps.

There are two main sources of fresh water—surface water and groundwater. Surface water includes water in lakes, ponds, rivers, and streams.

Groundwater is the water that collects in spaces and soil underground. Dig deep enough in any spot on land, and you'll reach groundwater.

Surface water is the easiest fresh water to get, but groundwater makes up most of Earth's usable fresh water supply. Groundwater must be pumped to the surface.

4. Complete the Venn diagram to compare surface water and groundwater.

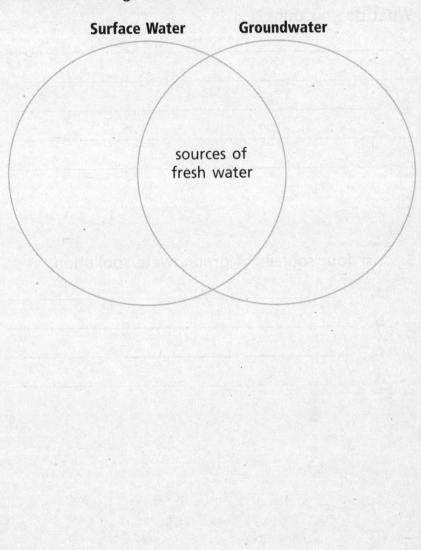

Surface Water   Groundwater

sources of fresh water

I Wonder . . . Why is the amount of rain that falls on Earth's surface different in different places? What do you think?

_____

_____

_____

_____

5. List four sources of groundwater pollution.

a. _____

b. _____

c. _____

d. _____

Fresh water is not spread out evenly over Earth's surface. The amount of rain is different in different places.

In places where there is a lot of fresh water, pollution can harm the water supply. Groundwater can also be polluted. Chemicals sink into groundwater from garbage dumps, factories, farms, and city streets.

Once fresh water becomes polluted, it can be very hard to clean up. Fresh water is an important resource that needs to be protected.

Lakes and rivers hold some of Earth's fresh water. Most of Earth's usable fresh water comes from groundwater.

REVERSE OSMOSIS Salt is trapped behind a membrane in reverse osmosis.

Fresh Water from the Sea

Ocean water can be changed into fresh water at a desalination plant. **Desalination** (dee sal uh NAY shuhn) is taking salt from salt water to make fresh water.

Distillation is one way to take the salt out of water. Water is heated and hot water evaporates. It becomes water vapor. The solid salt is left behind.

Reverse osmosis is another way to desalinate water. Water is pumped through membranes that trap dissolved salts.

Desalination costs a lot and it makes a salty waste that can pollute groundwater.

COMPARE AND CONTRAST

What is the most important difference between ocean water and fresh water?

Summary Most of Earth's water is salt water found in the oceans. List two ways to desalinate water so that people can get fresh water from ocean water.

a. _____

b. _____

Compare and Contrast What is the most important difference between ocean water and fresh water?

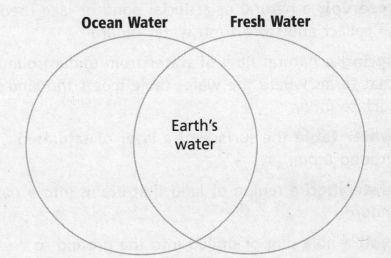

Ocean Water   Fresh Water

Earth's water

VOCABULARY

aqueduct a system of channels, pipes, or tunnels that carry water a long distance *(noun)*

aquifer an underground layer of rock or soil through which water easily moves *(noun)*

irrigation the process of supplying fresh water to farm fields for growing crops *(noun)*

reservoir a natural or artificial pond or lake used to collect and store fresh water *(noun)*

spring a natural flow of water from underground that forms where the water table meets the land's surface *(noun)*

water table the surface of a layer of saturated ground *(noun)*

watershed a region of land that drains into a river *(noun)*

well a hole dug or drilled into the ground to provide a supply of water *(noun)*

3.d. Students know that fresh water is a limited resource.
3.e. Students know where the water used by their community comes from.

2 How Do Communities Get Water?

Communities get water from places underground and on Earth's surface.

Rivers and Reservoirs

Rivers give drinking water to millions of Californians. The Colorado River gives water to people in southern California. The San Joaquin-Sacramento River gives water to central California.

Rivers are not reliable sources of fresh water. That means you cannot always count on them. Not all of the rain and snow that falls in California fills rivers and lakes. In hot, dry areas, water evaporates. Some water is lost when it soaks into the ground or is taken up by plant roots.

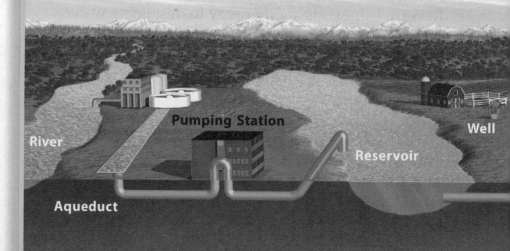

River
Pumping Station
Well
Reservoir
Aqueduct

The state of California has built many dams. It has also created reservoirs to make runoff from rain and snow last throughout the year. A **reservoir** (REZ uh vwahr) is a place that collects and holds water.

Fresh water is not always close to people who need it. Aqueducts are used to move water from faraway places. An **aqueduct** (AK wuh duct) is a system of channels, pipes, and tunnels that carries water a long distance.

Reservoirs, wells, and aqueducts provide water to Californians.

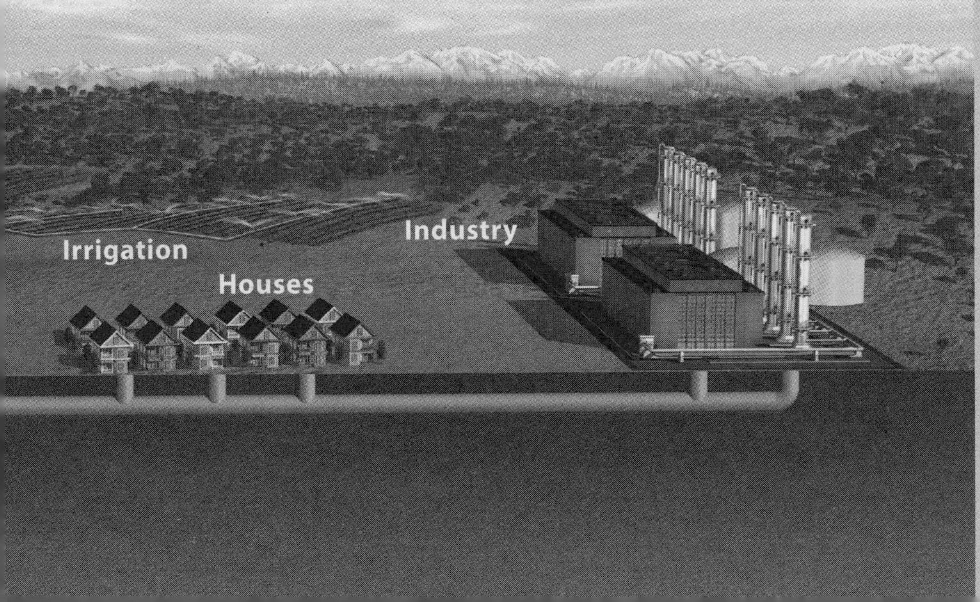

Irrigation

Industry

Houses

1. List three reasons why rivers are not reliable sources of fresh water in California.

a. _____

_____

b. _____

_____

c. _____

_____

2. Use the diagram to list the parts of California's system for supplying fresh water to homes and industry.

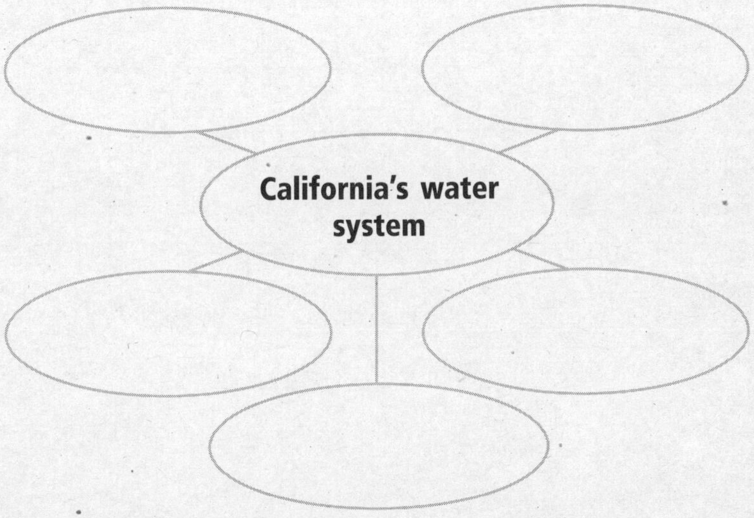

California's water system

3. Complete the chart to describe why and how California provides water for irrigation of crops.

Most rain and snow falls between _____ and _____. Crops need to be watered in _____ and _____.

↓

_____ and _____ help collect and hold the water.

↓

Water is used for _____ of crops in _____ and _____.

Most rain and snow in California falls between October and April. Crops need to be watered in the spring and summer. Reservoirs and aqueducts help collect water that can be used for irrigation. **Irrigation** is the supplying of fresh water to farm fields. Irrigation systems are like small-scale aqueducts.

Dams have other uses, too. Water rushing past dams can be used to make electricity. People can boat, swim, or fish on the reservoirs they form.

Groundwater

Groundwater supplies drinking water to less than half of the people in California. The source of most groundwater is rain and melted snow that sinks into the ground. The water sinks down until it reaches a layer of solid rock or hard clay. Water cannot sink any further. It fills the spaces above this layer.

An underground layer of rock or soil that water can easily move through is an **aquifer** (AK wih fuhr). When all the spaces are filled with water, the ground is saturated, or soaked.

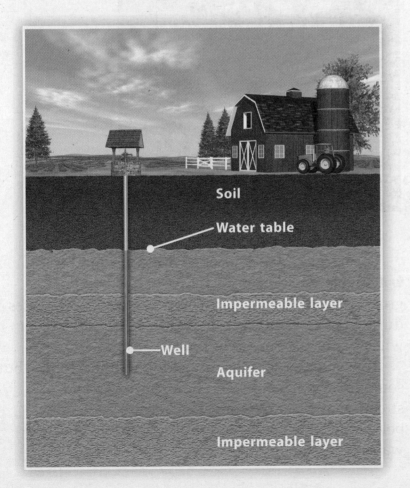

4. Circle the correct answer.
   In California, groundwater supplies drinking water to (more than two-thirds, less than half) of the people.

5. Complete each sentence to tell about aquifers.

   a. The source of most groundwater in
      California is _____ and
      _____.

   b. Water sinks into the ground. The water is
      stopped by a layer of _____ or
      _____.

   c. Look at the picture. Circle the layers that
      stop water from sinking. What is another
      name for these layers?

      _____

6. Complete the diagram to tell what causes the water table to rise and fall.

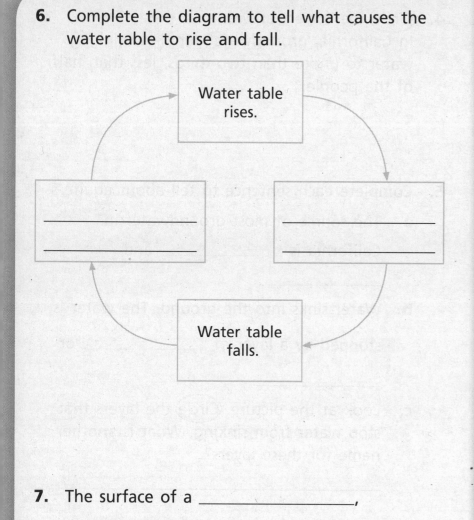

Water table rises.

_____
_____

_____
_____

Water table falls.

7. The surface of a _____,
_____, or _____
may be at the same level as the water table.

90

Digging a well is a simple way to supply fresh water.

The surface of a layer of saturated ground is the **water table**. That means it is the soaked layer of ground just above groundwater. The water table rises during heavy rainfall. It sinks during dry periods or when water is pumped out of the ground.

The water table is usually hidden underground, but sometimes you can see it. The surface of a lake or stream may be at the same level as the water table below the land. A wetland is also at the level of the water table.

People often get to groundwater by drilling down into aquifers. A **well** is a hole dug or drilled under ground to a place filled with water.

Pumps are used to bring water up to the surface. In artesian wells, water flows to the surface without the use of pumps. Pumping water from under the surface can make a well run dry. It can also sink the land.

People sometimes get water from springs. A **spring** is a natural flow of water from below the ground.

A spring in a desert forms an oasis. The oasis supplies water to plants and animals that could not survive without it.

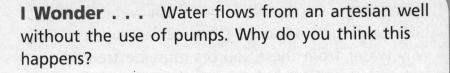

I Wonder . . .   Water flows from an artesian well without the use of pumps. Why do you think this happens?

_____

_____

_____

_____

_____

_____

Summary Communities get fresh water from both underground sources and surface sources. Tell why water from these sources must be treated before it is safe to drink.

_____

_____

_____

Main Idea and Details How do people get fresh water from an aquifer?

Main Idea:
People can get fresh water from an aquifer.

Detail:
People drill

_____

and

_____

water to the surface.

Detail:
Water can flow from

_____

and from

_____

wells.

Water to You

A **watershed** is a piece of land that drains into a river. Your drinking water may come from a watershed.

Water from a river or lake is not always clean and safe to drink. It must be treated, or cleaned, at a purification plant.

Water is treated with chlorine and other chemicals that kill bacteria. The water is also cleaned before it is sent into the community. Used, dirty water goes into the sewer system. Then it goes to a water treatment plant.

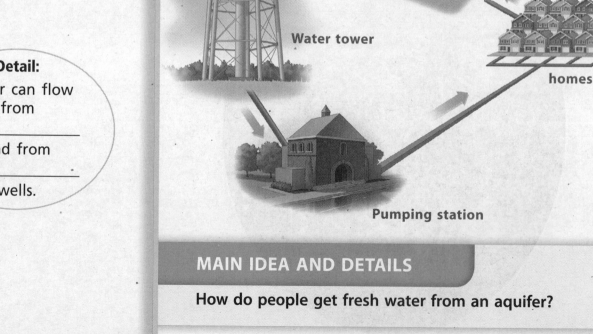

Water treatment plant

Water tower

homes

Pumping station

MAIN IDEA AND DETAILS

How do people get fresh water from an aquifer?

How Can Fresh Water Be Used Wisely?

3

Water should be conserved so fresh water supplies will last longer.

California's Water Needs

California has the largest population of any U.S. state. California is also the country's leading farming state.

The people and farms of California need huge amounts of fresh water. But the people and farms are not always close to the state's big water supplies.

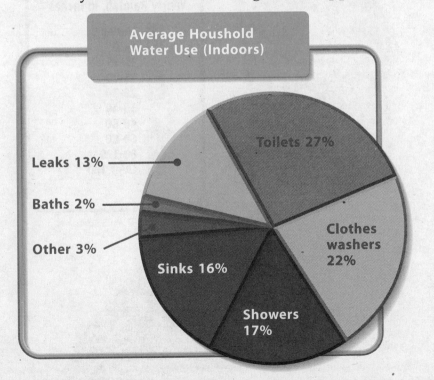

Average Houshold Water Use (Indoors)

- Toilets 27%
- Leaks 13%
- Baths 2%
- Other 3%
- Sinks 16%
- Clothes washers 22%
- Showers 17%

VOCABULARY

conservation the careful use of a natural resource, such as water *(noun)*

water reclamation the recycling of waste water so it can be used again *(noun)*

VOCABULARY SKILL: Word Roots

Look at the words *conservation* and *reclamation*. What shorter words do you think they are based on? Use a dictionary if you need help.

_____

_____

 3.d. Students know that fresh water is a limited resource.

1. List two reasons that California needs huge amounts of fresh water.

a. _____

b. _____

2. Look at the map. (Circle) the regions of California that get less than 10 inches of rain each year.

The average yearly rainfall and snowfall in California is about 58 centimeters (23 inches). Most of this precipitation falls in areas of the state that have fewer people.

Only about one-third of the rain falls in the central valley and southern California. These places are home to most of the state's people, cities, and farms.

The state works to get water to everyone. The San Joaquin Valley and southern California get less than 10 inches of rain each year. This is not enough to give water to the people there.

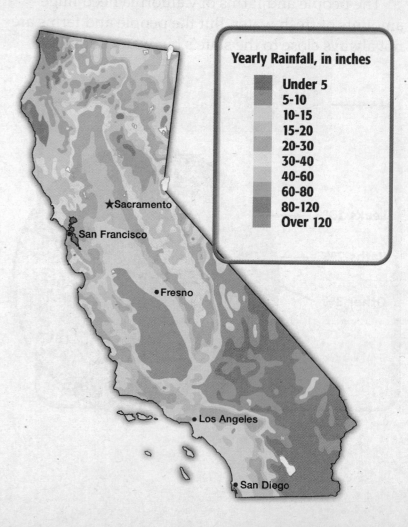

Yearly Rainfall, in inches

Under 5
5-10
10-15
15-20
20-30
30-40
40-60
60-80
80-120
Over 120

★Sacramento

San Francisco

Fresno

Los Angeles

San Diego

Most California farms use irrigation systems to water crops.

A huge system of canals, pipes, aqueducts, dams, pumps, and reservoirs brings water to places where it is needed. Water is moved from the wet north to the dry south. This means most Californians can live and farm in places that would not have enough water for them.

Now Californians are starting to need more water than they have. New steps are being taken so that everyone has the water they need.

3. Complete the diagram to describe the path by which water flows through California.

From the wet _____

water is moved through a huge system of

_____, _____, _____,

_____, _____, and

_____.

to the dry _____.

4. Tell what bringing water to places where it is needed has allowed Californians to do.

_____

_____

_____

5. Look at the map. Circle the aqueduct that connects the San Francisco area and Los Angeles.

Sharing Water

About 100 years ago, Californians began to use huge systems to move water. The Los Angeles Aqueduct brings water over the mountains from Owens Valley. This aqueduct supplies about 80 percent of Los Angeles's water.

Most of the water Californians use today comes from two main sources—the Sacramento-San Joaquin River and the Colorado River. About 1,300 dams and reservoirs and 6 major aqueduct systems move the water from wetter areas to drier areas.

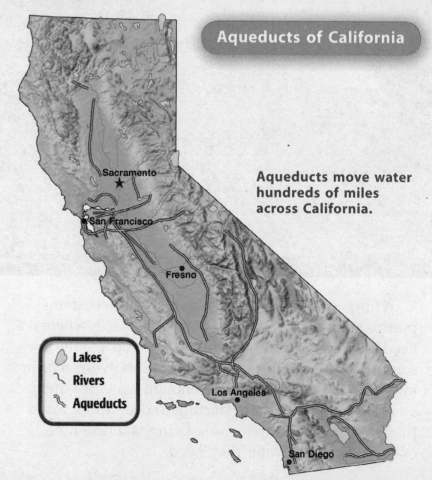

Aqueducts of California

Aqueducts move water hundreds of miles across California.

Lakes
Rivers
Aqueducts

The Colorado River is an important source of fresh water for many states.

Six other states and a part of Mexico share the water of the Colorado River. Each state gets some of the river's water each year. But in the 1990s, California used more than its share. California was borrowing some of the water from other states.

The other states did not need all the water they could have. But now the number of people in states such as Arizona and Nevada has grown. They need the additional water. California can no longer take more than its share from the Colorado River.

6. Who shares the water of the Colorado River?

_____

_____

7. Explain why California can no longer take more than its share of water from the Colorado River.

The number of _____ in states such

as _____ and _____ has

grown. Now those states need additional

_____.

I Wonder . . . One way that Plan 4.4 hopes to reduce the need for water in California is by asking farmers to stop growing crops in certain places. How might the fact that California is located next to the Pacific Ocean help with water supply needs in the future?

_____

_____

_____

_____

_____

_____

The Federal government and the states sharing water reached an agreement in 2000. The agreement is called the 4.4 Plan, and it backs laws that cut down water usage. California must use only the water it is allowed by 2015.

The 4.4 Plan asks everyone to help save water. Canals will be lined to stop leaks. Farmers are asked to stop growing crops in certain places and to use water-saving irrigation methods.

There is a limit on the amount of fresh water that can be shared every year. California's water needs will continue to be an important issue.

This aqueduct is in California's Central Valley. It brings water to people and crops.

Conserving Water

The careful use of a natural resource such as fresh water is called **conservation**. Conservation of a resource will help it last longer.

Most of California's water is used to help farms. A lot of water can be saved by watering these farms wisely. Some people flood farm fields with water. This wastes water.

A new way of watering the farms is called drip irrigation. Drip irrigation uses much less water and most of the water reaches the crops.

Water conservation helps community gardens and parks use water wisely.

8. Complete the diagram to compare methods of watering crops.

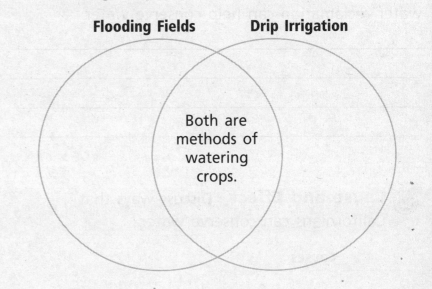

Flooding Fields   **Drip Irrigation**

Both are methods of watering crops.

Summary   Water should be conserved in order to make fresh water supplies last longer. Explain how water reclamation can help conserve water.

_____

_____

_____

_____

Cause and Effect   Discuss ways that Californians can conserve water.

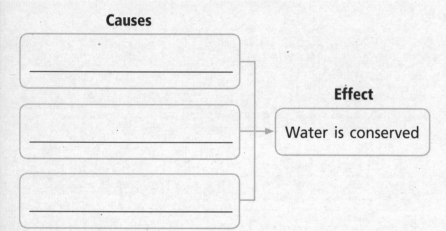

Causes

Effect

Water is conserved

California has also passed laws to help people with water conservation. One law addresses **water reclamation**, the recycling of waste water so it can be used again. Between 50 and 75 percent of waste water can be used to water lawns or plants, or to wash floors and cars.

Other laws ask people to replace old toilets with new toilets that use less water. This change can save millions of liters of water each year!

You can conserve water, too. Study the list of tips below to see what you can do.

Tips for Saving Water

- Run only full loads in dish and clothes washers.

- To wash dishes, fill the sink or basin with water. Don't let the faucet run.

- Turn off water while brushing your teeth.

- Take shorter showers. Just one or two minutes less can save up to 3,000 liters a month.

- Install low-flow toilets and shower heads.

- Keep a bottle of cold drinking water in the refrigerator. Don't waste water by running the tap.

CAUSE AND EFFECT

Discuss ways that Californians can conserve water.

aqueduct (AK wuh dukt) a system of channels, pipes, or tunnels that carry water a long distance

acueducto sistema de canales, tuberías o túneles que transportan agua a grandes distancias

aquifer (AK wuh fur) an underground layer of rock or soil through which water easily moves

acuífero capa subterránea de roca o suelo a través de la cual el agua se mueve fácilmente

conservation the careful use of a natural resource, such as water

conservación uso prudente de un recurso natural, como el agua

desalination (dee sal uh NAY shuhn) the removal of salt from salt water to make fresh water

desalinización eliminación de la sal del agua marina para hacer agua potable

groundwater water that collects in spaces and cracks in rocks and soil underground

agua subterránea agua que se acumula en los espacios y grietas de las rocas y del suelo subterráneo

irrigation the process of supplying fresh water to farm fields for growing crops

riegoproceso mediante el cual se suministra agua dulce a los campos agrícolas para su cultivos

Circle the three-syllable words on the page.

Visit www.eduplace.com to play puzzles and word games.

Draw a box around the Spanish words that have *agua* as part of the term. What is the English word for *agua*?

_____

Glossary

reservoir (REZ uh vwahr) a natural or artificial pond or lake used to collect and store fresh water

embalse lago natural o artificial que se usa para recoger y almacenar agua dulce

runoff rainwater that flows over land without sinking into the soil

escurrimiento agua de lluvia que fluye por la tierra sin penetrar en el suelo

spring a natural flow of water from underground that forms where the water table meets the land's surface

manantial corriente natural de agua subterránea que aparece donde el nivel hidrostático se une con la superficie de la tierra

water reclamation the recycling of waste water so it can be used again

recuperación del agua reciclaje de agua residual para que pueda usarse de nuevo

water table the surface of a layer of saturated ground

nivel hidrostático superficie de una capa de suelo saturada de agua

watershed a region of land that drains into a river

divisoria de aguas zona cuyas aguas desembocan en un mismo río

well a hole dug or drilled into the ground to provide a supply of water

pozo hoyo excavado o taladrado en el suelo para proporcionar suministro de agua

Responding

Think About What You Have Read

Vocabulary

❶ A natural flow of water from underground to the surface is a/an _____.

A) reservoir

B) spring

C) well

D) watershed

Comprehension

❷ How are distillation and reverse osmosis alike? How are they different?

❸ What are the main goals of water purification?

❹ How is California's water use changing?

Critical Thinking

❺ Although 70 percent of Earth's surface is covered by water, it is still considered to be a limited resource. Explain.

K W L

WHAT DID YOU LEARN?

Vocabulary

❶ Circle the correct answer on the page.

Comprehension

❷ _____

_____

_____

_____

❸ _____

_____

❹ _____

_____

_____

Critical Thinking

❺ _____

_____

_____

_____

WHAT DO YOU KNOW?

List one fact about each of these topics:

a. How water changes state _____

_____

_____

b. How precipitation forms _____

_____

_____

c. How the ocean affects weather _____

_____

_____

The Water Cycle

Contents

WHAT DO YOU WANT TO KNOW?

Skim the pictures and headings in this chapter. List one thing you want to find out about each of these topics:

a. Water changing state _____

_____

_____

_____

b. Different forms of precipitation _____

_____

_____

_____

c. The effects of ocean waters on weather _____

_____

_____

_____

VOCABULARY

condensation the change of state from a gas to a liquid *(noun)*

evaporation the change in state from a liquid to a gas; slow or gradual vaporization *(noun)*

precipitation any form of water that falls to Earth's surface from clouds *(noun)*

transpiration the evaporation of water through a plant's leaves *(noun)*

water vapor water in the form of a gas *(noun)*

VOCABULARY SKILL: Word Forms

You can see that the terms *evaporation* and *water vapor* both include the term *vapor*. Think about what *evaporation* means and what *water vapor* means. Write your own definition of *vapor*. Then write what you think the word *vaporize* means.

_____

_____

_____

3.a. Students know that most of Earth's water is salty and is found in oceans. Oceans cover most of Earth's surface.
3.c Students know that water exists as a gas in the air. This water can move from place to place and change to a liquid or ice and fall to Earth.

1 How Does Water Change State?

Water is found in three states on Earth: water, ice, and a gas called water vapor. Water changes from one state to another in different parts of the water cycle.

Water in the Environment

Rain is very important for all life. It is part of the water cycle. The water cycle is a process that brings water to Earth. The water cycle also cleans Earth's water supply.

Water moves from Earth's surface into the air and back to the surface again in the water cycle.

CONDENSATION
Cooled water vapor condenses. It becomes water droplets and forms clouds.

EVAPORATION
Heat from the Sun causes evaporation. Water from oceans, lakes, and rivers evaporates. Water vapor rises in the air and cools.

There are three states of water: ice, water, and water vapor. **Water vapor** (VAY pur) is water in the form of gas. Water changes between states as it is heated or cooled.

Energy from the Sun causes liquid water to evaporate from Earth's surface. During **evaporation** (ih vap uh RAY shuhn), liquids change to the gas state.

Water vapor is also put into the atmosphere by plants. In **transpiration** (tran spuh RAY shuhn), the leaves of plants release water vapor into the air.

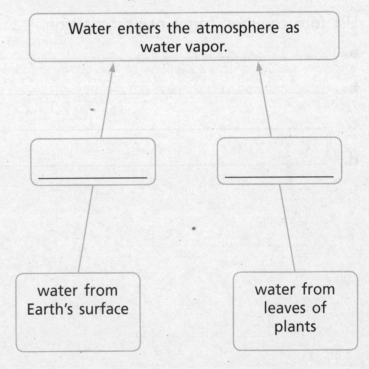

PRECIPITATION
Water droplets in the clouds become heavy. They fall as precipitation.

1. List the three states of water.

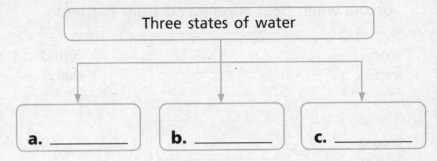

Three states of water

a. _____ b. _____ c. _____

2. Identify the ways in which water vapor gets into the atmosphere.

Water enters the atmosphere as water vapor.

_____   _____

water from Earth's surface   water from leaves of plants

3. Tell the name of each change of state that occurs when heat is removed from matter.

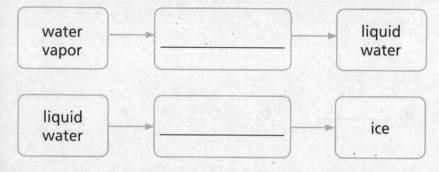

water vapor → _____ → liquid water

liquid water → _____ → ice

4. List four common forms of precipitation.

a. _____

b. _____

c. _____

d. _____

Water returns to Earth's surface as precipitation.

Water vapor condenses back into a liquid when it cools. **Condensation** (kahn dehn SAY shuhn) is the change of state from a gas to a liquid. More cooling can cause freezing. Freezing is the change from liquid to solid.

Water drops or ice crystals grow heavy and fall to Earth as precipitation. **Precipitation** (prih sihp uh TAY shuhn) is any form of water that falls to Earth's surface from clouds. It is usually rain, sleet, snow, or hail.

Groundwater and Runoff

Precipitation falls on land and some of it soaks into the ground. This water is called groundwater.

Runoff is water that flows downhill across Earth's surface. It does not sink into the ground. Runoff may flow into rivers, lakes, and streams.

Runoff causes erosion. The moving water picks up rocks and soil and carries them along to other places. Runoff can also pick up harmful chemicals. These chemicals can seep into groundwater.

Runoff may flow after heavy rains. Erosion from runoff may form trenches, called gullies.

Summary On Earth, water exists in three states: liquid water, solid ice, and a gas called water vapor. In a process called the water cycle, water changes from one state to another. Describe each part of the water cycle.

Evaporation: _____

_____

Condensation: _____

_____

Precipitation: _____

_____

 Compare and Contrast Explain the difference between runoff and groundwater.

Groundwater   Runoff

Precipitation that falls on land

109

Lesson Preview

VOCABULARY

convection current a continuous loop of moving air or liquid that transfers energy *(noun)*

dew point the temperature at which air becomes saturated *(noun)*

humidity the amount of water vapor in the air at any given time *(noun)*

VOCABULARY SKILL: Word Roots

Humidity is a noun based on the adjective *humid*. What is the weather like when people say that it is a humid day?

_____

_____

_____

3.b. Students know that water can change states in the atmosphere.
3.c. Students know that water exists as a gas in the air. This water can move from place to place and change to a liquid or ice and fall to Earth.

2 How Does Precipitation Form?

Clouds form and release precipitation as rain, snow, sleet, and hail.

Cloud Formation

The Sun warms Earth's surface. The air just above the surface warms, too. Warm air rises. It is cooler above Earth's surface, so the warm air cools slowly. The cold air sinks back to the ground.

This is called convection. A **convection current** is a loop of moving air or liquid that transfers energy.

Convection Currents

Colder air begins to sink.

Water condenses as air cools, forming a cloud.

Warm, moist air rises.

Cloud Types

Cirrus	Stratus	Cumulus	Cumulonimbus
• Thin, wispy clouds at high altitude • Made of ice crystals • Indicate pleasant weather that may change to rain	• Form in layers • May cover large parts of the sky • Some bring rain	• Puffy, white clouds with flat bottoms • Form in currents of air • Generally mean fair weather	• Bring heavy rain or thunderstorms • May extend up through the atmosphere

Warm air carries more water vapor than cool air. Warm air in a convection current carries water vapor with it. The water vapor then forms tiny drops of water. These water drops can remain in the air, forming clouds.

Cloud Types

Scientists once thought clouds had no form. Luke Howard studied clouds as a hobby. He described four classes of clouds. This way of naming clouds is still in use today. The photos above show Howard's four basic cloud types.

1. Look at the diagram of convection currents. What will happen to the colder air at the top of the clouds?

   _____

   _____

2. Draw a line under the correct answer. Warm air carries (more, less) water vapor than cool air does.

3. Identify and describe the four basic cloud types.

Cloud Types

4. Tell how each type of precipitation forms.

Type of Precipitation	How It Forms
Rain	
Sleet	
Snow	

Forms of Precipitation

All kinds of precipitation fall from clouds. The kind of precipitation that will fall depends on what it is like inside the clouds and what it is like in the air.

Rain Drops of liquid water are rain. Rain is the most common form of precipitation. Rain forms when tiny cloud drops combine. A great number of these drops must combine to form a raindrop that is large enough and heavy enough to fall to the ground.

Rain is falling drops of liquid water.

Sleet This kind of precipitation begins as small drops of rain. The raindrops fall through a layer of air that is colder than water's freezing point. This causes the raindrops to freeze into tiny balls of ice. These balls of ice reach the ground as sleet.

Snow Small flakes and balls of ice make up snow. Sometimes the temperature in a cloud is cold enough for water vapor to turn into ice crystals. When this happens, a snowflake is formed. Cold temperatures make light, fluffy snowflakes. Warmer temperatures make heavy, wet flakes.

Sleet forms when rain freezes as it falls.

5. Explain how temperature affects the type of snowflakes that form.

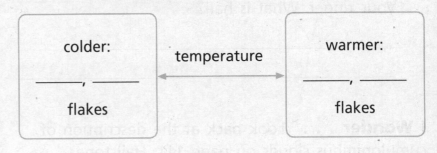

colder:

——, ——

flakes

temperature

warmer:

——, ——

flakes

I Wonder . . . Some regions can have *freezing* rain. This is precipitation that falls as rain but coats surfaces with ice. What conditions may cause freezing rain? What do you think?

_____

_____

_____

_____

_____

113

6. Look at the picture of hail formation on this page. Follow the path of the hailstones with your finger. What is hail?

_____

_____

I Wonder . . . Look back at the description of cumulonimbus clouds on page 111. Hailstones usually form in this kind of cloud. Why is this so? What do you think?

_____

_____

_____

Hail Round chunks of ice called hailstones fall to the ground as hail. Hailstones form when drops of rain freeze inside a cloud with strong winds. The winds lift the hailstone through the inside of the cloud.

A hailstone may rise and fall many times within the cloud. Each time it gains a new icy coat. The hailstone grows too heavy for the wind to lift, and it falls to the ground.

Hail Formation

Cumulonimbus cloud

Cold Air

A strong updraft in a cloud can make a large hailstone.

Freezing Air 0°C

Warm Air

Strong Updrafts

Rain Forest

Desert

The air temperature may be the same in a rain forest and a desert. It is the humidity that makes all the difference.

Humidity

The amount of water vapor in the air can change. **Humidity** is the amount of water vapor in the air at any one time.

Humidity can change because the temperature changes. Warm air can hold more water vapor than cold air can.

Relative humidity is the amount of water vapor in the air compared to the greatest amount it can hold at that temperature. The temperature at which air becomes saturated is its **dew point**. The air temperature can drop below the dew point. When this happens, water condenses and clouds form.

SEQUENCE

Describe the stages in the formation of a hailstone.

Summary   Clouds form and release precipitation as rain, snow, sleet, and hail. Tell how *humidity* and *relative humidity* are related.

_____

_____

_____

_____

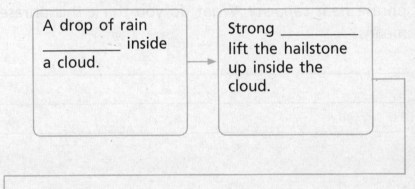

Sequence   Describe the stages in the formation of a hailstone.

A drop of rain _____ inside a cloud.

Strong _____ lift the hailstone up inside the cloud.

Each time it rises and falls, the hailstone _____.

The hailstone _____ for wind to lift it and falls to the ground.

VOCABULARY

ocean current a moving stream of water in the ocean *(noun)*

VOCABULARY SKILL: Word Phrases

In this lesson, you will read about heat capacity. The word *capacity* means "the ability to contain, absorb, or receive and hold." Think about the phrase *heat capacity.* What do you think this phrase means?

_____

_____

_____

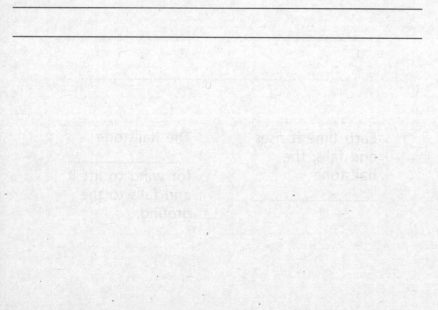

4.a. Students know that uneven heating of Earth's surface causes air movements.
4.b. Students know that the oceans affect weather.

---

3 How Does the Ocean Affect Weather?

Oceans have a major effect on Earth's weather and climate.

Heating Land and Water

The Sun shines equally on the water and the concrete walkway in the photograph on this page. But the water is much cooler than the concrete because they have different heat capacities. This means that the two materials heat up and cool down at different rates.

Land and water have different specific heat capacities. Land heats up faster and reaches higher temperatures than the bodies of water near land. Land areas also lose heat more quickly and drop to lower temperatures.

Cold Water

Hot Cement

Water in the pool heats up more slowly than the land around it.

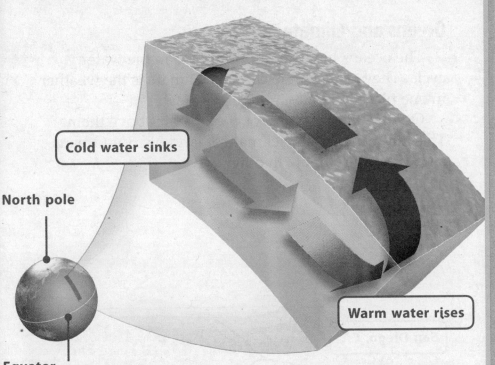

Cold water sinks

North pole

Equator

Warm water rises

DEEP OCEAN CURRENTS Ocean currents move hot and cold water around Earth's oceans. Oceans help keep the weather on nearby land even.

Ocean Currents

An **ocean current** is a moving stream of water in the ocean. Water in a current has a set temperature.

There are two kinds of ocean currents. They are called surface currents and deep currents. The graphic above shows warm and cold currents.

These currents move in big circles. Warm currents move warm ocean water from warm places to cold places. Cold currents move in the other direction. These currents help the temperatures at Earth's surface stay even.

1. **Circle** the correct words to make each statement *true*.

   a. Land and water have (different, the same) specific heat capacities.

   b. Land heats up (faster, slower) and reaches (higher, lower) temperatures than bodies of water that are near land.

   c. Land loses heat (faster, slower) than water does.

2. Complete each statement about the direction in which ocean currents flow by underlining the correct words.

   a. (Cold, Warm) currents move (cold, warm) ocean water from (cold, warm) places to cold places.

   b. (Cold, warm) currents move in the opposite direction.

I Wonder . . . Ocean currents warm or cool the air above them. This air influences the climate of land nearby. What would the effect on Earth's climate be if ocean currents stopped flowing? What do you think?

_____

_____

_____

_____

3. Look at the graph on the next page. Compare the average monthly temperatures for the two cities. Why is the line for San Diego much flatter than the line for Dallas?

_____

_____

_____

_____

Oceans and Climate

The oceans have an important job in the water cycle. They also change climate. Climate is the weather in one place over a long time.

Ocean currents warm or cool the air above them. This air influences the climate of land nearby. Oceans also affect the climate in other ways.

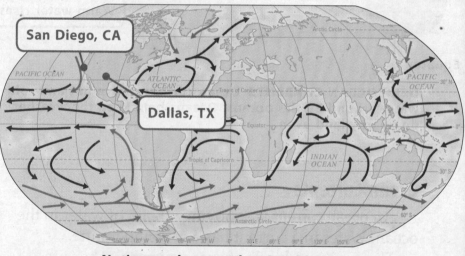

Notice on the map that San Diego is closer to the ocean than Dallas.

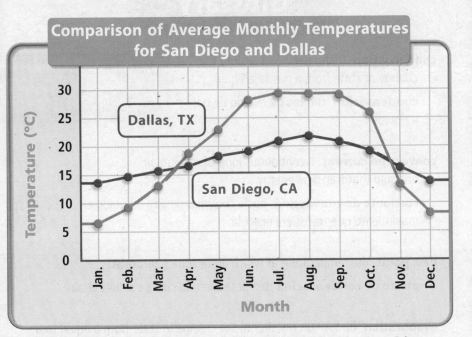

Comparison of Average Monthly Temperatures for San Diego and Dallas

Temperature (°C)

Dallas, TX

San Diego, CA

Month

Being closer to the ocean makes the weather in San Diego milder than in Dallas.

Water heats up and cools down more slowly than land. Oceans hold the heat of summer long into winter. The land nearby has cooled, but the ocean slowly lets out the stored energy into the air. Oceans warm the nearby lands. The land does not get as cold as it would without the ocean.

The opposite happens in the summer. Ocean waters warm more slowly than the land. The oceans stay cooler. This helps to keep land near the ocean cool in summer.

MAIN IDEA

How do land and water heat differently?

Summary Oceans have a major effect on Earth's weather and climate. Explain how ocean currents affect temperatures in different parts of Earth.

_____

_____

_____

_____

Main Idea How do land and water heat differently?

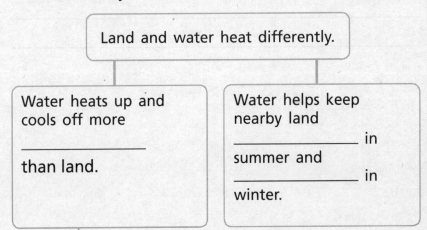

Land and water heat differently.

| Water heats up and cools off more _____ than land. | Water helps keep nearby land _____ in summer and _____ in winter. |

Glossary

Write a short paragraph that includes the words *condensation*, *evaporation*, and *precipitation*.

_____

_____

_____

_____

_____

_____

Glossary

condensation (kahn dehn SAY shuhn) the change of state from a gas to a liquid

condensación cambio de estado de gas a líquido

convection current a continuous loop of moving air or liquid that transfers energy

corriente de convección bucle continuo de aire o líquido en movimiento que transfiere energía

dew point the temperature at which air becomes saturated

punto de condensación temperatura a la cual se satura el aire

evaporation (ih VAP uh ray shuhn) the change in state from a liquid to a gas; slow or gradual vaporization

evaporación cambio de estado de líquido a gas; vaporización lenta o gradual

Glossary

humidity the amount of water vapor in the air at any given time

humedad cantidad de vapor de agua que hay en el aire en un momento determinado

ocean current a moving stream of water in the ocean

corriente oceánica corriente de agua en el océano

precipitation (prih sihp uh TAY shuhn) any form of water that falls to Earth's surface from clouds

precipitación agua proveniente de las nubes que, en cualquiera de sus formas, cae sobre la superficie de la Tierra

transpiration the evaporation of water through a plant's leaves

transpiración evaporación del agua a través de las hojas de una planta

water vapor (VAY pur) water in the form of a gas

vapor de agua agua en forma de gas

Visit www.eduplace.com to play puzzles and word games.

Find the English words that are like these Spanish words. List the English words in the chart.

Spanish Words	English Words
condensación	
evaporación	
humedad	
precipitación	

Chapter Review

KWL

WHAT DID YOU LEARN?

Vocabulary

❶ (Circle) the correct answer on the page.

Comprehension

❷ _____

_____

❸ _____

_____

_____

_____

❹ _____

_____

Critical Thinking

❺ _____

_____

_____

Think About What You Have Read

Vocabulary

❶ The change of state from a gas to a liquid is called _____.

A) evaporation

B) water vapor

C) condensation

D) precipitation

Comprehension

❷ How does water enter the atmosphere? How does it leave?

❸ What are the steps in the formation of a cloud?

❹ How do oceans affect the temperature of land areas near them?

Critical Thinking

❺ Why do so few clouds form in the skies above a desert?

Weather

KWL

WHAT DO YOU KNOW?

Think about different kinds of weather. What do you know about air pressure and weather?

_____

_____

_____

What do you know about how air moves?

_____

_____

_____

What do you know about how weather forecasts are made?

_____

_____

_____

What do you know about what causes storms?

_____

_____

_____

Contents

WHAT DO YOU WANT TO KNOW?
Look at the contents of this chapter. Then skim the pictures and headings in the chapter. List one thing you want to find out about each of these subjects.

a. Air pressure and how it affects weather

_____

_____

b. Why air moves

_____

_____

c. Predicting weather

_____

_____

d. What causes storms

_____

_____

VOCABULARY

air pressure the force exerted by air in all directions on a given area *(noun)*

atmosphere a mixture of gases that surround a planet *(noun)*

weather what the atmosphere is like at a given time and place *(noun)*

VOCABULARY SKILL: Word Origins

Many English words come from Latin or Greek. The word *atmosphere* is a noun that comes from the Greek word *atmos*, meaning "vapor" or "gas," and the Latin word *sphaera*, meaning "sphere." If the atmosphere forms layers around Earth's surface, why is the atmosphere called a sphere?"

_____

_____

_____

1 How Does Air Pressure Affect Weather?

Earth's atmosphere is a mixture of gases that surround the planet. The atmosphere gives off a force, or pressure, that lessens the farther it gets from the surface.

Composition of the Atmosphere

Weather is what the atmosphere is like at a given time and place. Earth's **atmosphere** is a group of gases that circle it. What goes on in the atmosphere—the weather—can change from day to day.

The atmosphere is made up mostly of two gases, nitrogen and oxygen. Other gases are there, but in small amounts.

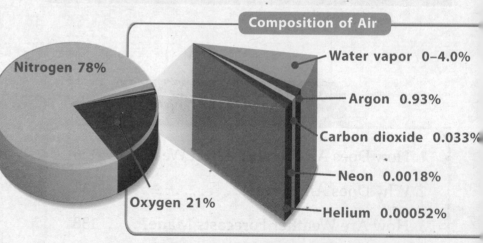

Composition of Air

Nitrogen 78%

Oxygen 21%

Water vapor 0–4.0%

Argon 0.93%

Carbon dioxide 0.033%

Neon 0.0018%

Helium 0.00052%

Air is mostly nitrogen and oxygen. Other gases are present in small amounts.

4.a. Students know that uneven heating of Earth's surface causes air movements.
4.e. Students know that the atmosphere pushes on Earth's surface.

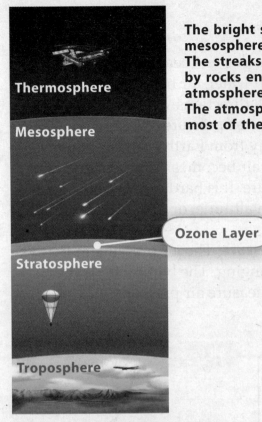

Thermosphere

The bright streaks in the mesosphere are meteors. The streaks are caused by rocks entering the atmosphere from space. The atmosphere burns most of them up.

Mesosphere

Ozone Layer

Stratosphere

Troposphere

Layers of the Atmosphere

Earth's atmosphere has four layers. The layer closest to Earth is the troposphere. Almost all weather happens here. It is the thinnest layer, but it has about three quarters of the atmosphere's air.

The stratosphere is above the troposphere. This layer has cold and dry air. It also has most of the planet's ozone, a form of oxygen. Ozone protects us from the Sun's rays.

The mesosphere is above the stratosphere. The top of this layer is the coldest part of the atmosphere. The level just above it, the thermosphere, is the first part of the atmosphere struck by sunlight. That makes it very hot—nearly 1,700 degrees Celsius.

1. Complete the table about the atmosphere. Write the name of the layer next to the fact that describes it.

Layer of the Atmosphere	Fact About the Layer
	It is the thinnest layer.
	It is the first part of the atmosphere struck by sunlight.
	The air here is very cold and dry.
	Most weather happens here.
	The coldest part of the atmosphere is in this layer.
	It has about three-quarters of Earth's air.
	It is just above the troposphere.
	It is the layer closest to Earth.
	Most of Earth's ozone is here.
	The temperature here is about 1,700 degrees Celsius.

2. What does the air pressure line graph on this page tell you?

_____

_____

I Wonder . . . The mountain climber in the photograph is carrying oxygen. Why do mountain climbers carry oxygen with them. What do you think?

_____

_____

_____

_____

_____

Air Pressure

The atmosphere is like an ocean of air around Earth. And like ocean water, air has mass and weight. It gives off force in all directions. The force given off by air on a place is the **air pressure**.

As you move away from Earth's surface, there is less and less air. The air becomes "thinner," meaning that it has less pressure. It is harder to breathe. So air pressure lessens with altitude, or distance above Earth's surface.

Measuring Air Pressure The air pressure at Earth's surface is always changing. The barometer is the instrument used to measure air pressure.

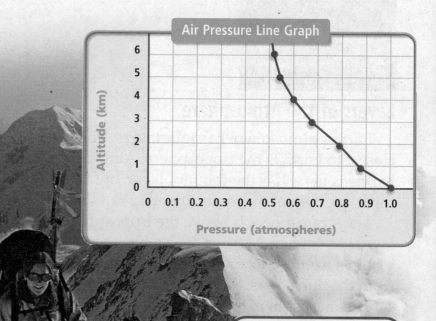

Air Pressure Line Graph

Altitude (km) vs. Pressure (atmospheres)

As altitude increases, the density of air decreases. This makes it harder to breathe.

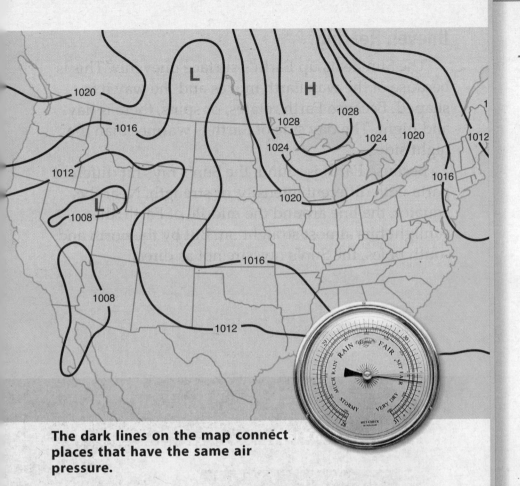

The dark lines on the map connect places that have the same air pressure.

Pressure Systems Air pressure at Earth's surface changes all the time. When the air at the surface rises, the air pressure goes down. A low-pressure system forms. In a low-pressure system, air moves toward the center of the system and then rises.

When air near the surface sinks, air pressure goes up. A high-pressure system forms. The air moves away from the center of the system.

High-pressure and low-pressure systems are closely linked to the weather you see.

3. What is a barometer?

_____

_____

4. What do the letters **L** and **H** on the map stand for?

_____

5. Compare pressure systems.

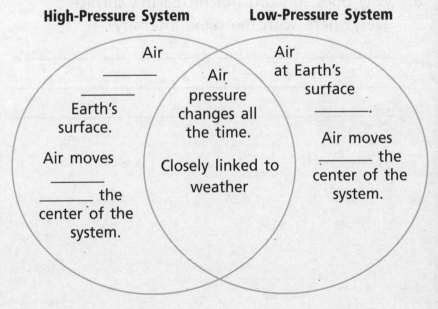

High-Pressure System

Low-Pressure System

Air

_____

_____

Earth's surface.

Air moves

_____

_____ the center of the system.

Air pressure changes all the time.

Closely linked to weather

Air at Earth's surface

_____.

Air moves _____ the center of the system.

129

6. Which side of Earth is cooler, the day side or the night side?

_____

7. Look at the picture on this page. What part of Earth is being hit by the Sun's rays with the least intensity?

_____

8. Why does sunlight not hit Earth's surface everywhere with the same intensity?

_____

_____

_____

Uneven Heating

The Sun heats up Earth's surface unevenly. This is because of the way Earth moves and the way it is shaped. Because Earth rotates, or spins, there is day and night. The day side of Earth is warmer than the night side.

Because Earth is round, the Sun's rays hit different parts with different intensity, or strength. Near the equator, the line around the middle of Earth, the sunlight hits almost straight on. But by the north and south poles, the Sun's rays are not as direct.

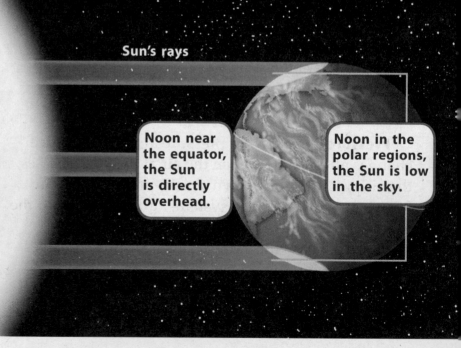

Sun's rays

Noon near the equator, the Sun is directly overhead.

Noon in the polar regions, the Sun is low in the sky.

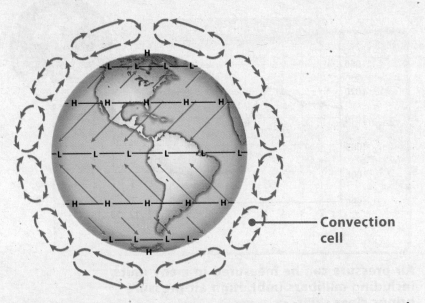

Uneven heating causes belts of high and low pressure and convection cells, or loops of rising and falling air.

Global Pressure Belts Uneven heating causes differences in air pressure. These differences affect weather all over the planet.

When air is warmed, it becomes less dense and rises. This makes a low-pressure system. When air is cooled, it becomes more dense, and it sinks. This makes a high-pressure system.

Uneven heating makes belts of high and low pressure. Belts circle Earth the same way they circle your waist. For example, the surface near the equator is always heated by the Sun. The warm air then rises and the pressure drops. As the map shows, the rising air forms a low-pressure belt near the equator.

The south and north poles are just the opposite. There, the Sun's rays do not hit the surface directly, so there is little heating of the air. The cold air sinks and cools, making a high-pressure belt.

9. Complete the diagrams that tell how high- and low-pressure systems form.

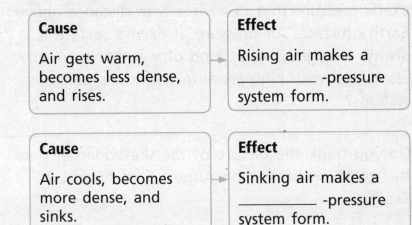

Cause	Effect
Air gets warm, becomes less dense, and rises.	Rising air makes a _____ -pressure system form.

Cause	Effect
Air cools, becomes more dense, and sinks.	Sinking air makes a _____ -pressure system form.

10. Would you expect to see areas of low pressure or high pressure over Earth's poles? Why?

_____

_____

_____

_____

Summary Earth's atmosphere is a mixture of gases that surrounds the planet. The atmosphere exerts pressure that decreases with distance above Earth's surface. Air pressure at Earth's surface is always changing. What kind of weather is usually associated with high-pressure and low-pressure systems?

Do you think the picture of the skateboarder near the graph was taken on August 5 or August 8? Explain.

Draw Conclusions Why does the air rise near the equator?

Text Clues	Prior Knowledge	Conclusion
When air gets warm, it becomes less dense and rises.		
Near the equator the sunlight hits almost straight on.		
The surface near the equator is always heated by the Sun.		

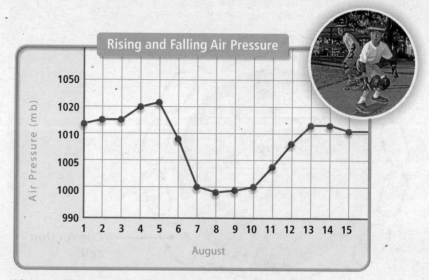

Rising and Falling Air Pressure

Air Pressure (mb)

1050
1020
1010
1005
1000
990

1 2 3 4 5 6 7 8 9 10 11 12 13 14 15

August

Air pressure can be measured in many units, including millibars (mb). High air pressure brings clear skies.

Air Pressure and Weather

Clouds form in a low-pressure system. Many times this leads to rain and storms. Low-pressure systems are a sign of bad weather.

Clouds cannot form in a high-pressure system. The sky stays clear. High-pressure systems are a sign of good weather.

People who predict the weather check the air pressure. A change in the air pressure can mean a change in the weather. But they check other things, too. It is important to know the temperature, the wind, and the humidity. Humidity is the amount of water that is in the air.

DRAW CONCLUSIONS

Why does the air rise near the equator?

Why Does Air Move?

Differences in air pressure make wind. These differences cause local winds and planetary winds.

Winds and Convection Currents

Wind is air moving across Earth's surface. The Sun heats Earth's surface, but the heating is not even. This causes differences in air pressure, which lead to winds. This means that the Sun causes the wind.

Winds blow harder at high altitudes, such as on mountains. That is because on the surface winds are slowed by trees, buildings, and other things that can block them. For the same reason, winds blow faster over smooth oceans than over hilly lands.

The wind that fills these sails is created by differences in air pressure.

VOCABULARY

jet stream narrow belt of high-speed winds in the upper troposphere *(noun)*

land breeze a local wind that blows at night from land toward water *(noun)*

mountain breeze a local wind that flows downhill and is produced by cooler, denser air above the mountain slopes *(noun)*

planetary winds long-lasting wind patterns that cover a large area of Earth *(noun)*

sea breeze a local wind that blows from water toward land during the day *(noun)*

valley breeze a local wind produced by the movement of cooler air from the valley that moves up a mountain slope *(noun)*

VOCABULARY SKILL: Word Parts

In this lesson you will read the word *windward*. The suffix *-ward* is added to a root word to show direction. For example, if someone told you to look skyward, you would know to look up. Write another word that ends with *-ward* and give its definition.

_____

_____

 4.a. Students know that uneven heating of Earth's surface causes air movements.
4.e. Students know that the atmosphere pushes on Earth's surface.

133

1. What is a convection current?

_____

_____

2. Complete the diagram to tell how a valley breeze forms.

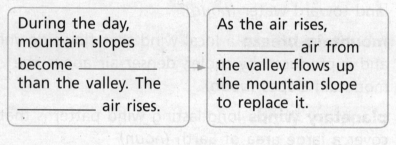

| During the day, mountain slopes become _____ than the valley. The _____ air rises. | → | As the air rises, _____ air from the valley flows up the mountain slope to replace it. |

3. Complete the diagram to tell how a mountain breeze forms.

| At night, air over the mountain slopes becomes _____ and more dense. | → | The _____, dense air from the slopes flows down into the valley. |

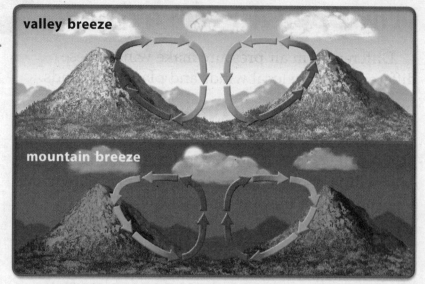

valley breeze

mountain breeze

Valley breezes blow up the mountain during the day. Mountain breezes blow down at night. Both breezes are part of convection currents.

Winds are kinds of convection currents. A convection current is a loop of air or water that carries energy. Some loops of wind, called local winds, cover small parts of the atmosphere. Global winds cover much larger parts.

Local winds include mountain breezes and valley breezes. During the day, the sides of mountains, or slopes, are heated up more than the valley is. As the warm air from the mountain rises, cool air from the valley rushes in to replace it. This is a **valley breeze**.

At night, the direction of the wind changes. The mountain cools quickly. This cool, dense air flows down the mountain into the valley. This is a **mountain breeze**.

Land and Sea Breezes

Have you ever been to the beach on a hot day and been surprised by how cold the water was? Then you know that land and water heat up and cool down at different speeds. This results in local winds called land breezes and sea breezes.

A **sea breeze** is a wind that blows from water to land during the day. Land heats faster than water. As warm air rises over the land, cool air moves in from the water to take its place.

At night, air moves in the opposite direction. Land cools faster than water, so the air over the water is now warmer. Cool air from the land moves in to replace the rising warm air. This movement of air from land toward water is a **land breeze**.

SEA BREEZE
A sea breeze flows from the water toward the land.

LAND BREEZE
A land breeze flows from the land toward the water.

4. Circle the words that correctly complete each sentence.

   a. (Land, water) heats more quickly than (land, water).

   b. (Land, water) cools more quickly than (land, water).

5. Use your finger to trace the convection currents on the diagrams of land and sea breezes. Then, in the chart below, identify each breeze by its description.

Type of Breeze	Description
_____ breeze	Warm air over land rises; cool air from over the water flows toward land.
_____ breeze	Warm air over water rises; cool air from land flows toward water.

135

6. (Circle) the windward side of the mountain.

7. Complete the diagram to tell about the mountain effect, or what happens to moving air when it comes to a mountain.

> Moist air comes to a mountain and is forced to rise.

↓

> The rising air _____.

↓

> _____ form, and it begins to _____ on the windward side of the mountain.

↓

> When the air gets to the other side of the mountain, it has little moisture left.

↓

> Winds going down the leeward side of the mountain are _____.

Mountain Effect

Moving air that comes to a mountain is forced to go up over the mountain. As the rising air cools, moisture in the air forms clouds. Rain falls on the side of the mountain where the air is rising and cooling. This is called the windward side of the mountain. Some of the wettest places on Earth are windward sides of mountains.

When the air finally gets to the other side of the mountain, it does not have any moisture left. Dry winds blow down the side of the mountain. This side is called the leeward side. Deserts are common on the

2. CONDENSATION The mountains force the moist air high into the atmosphere.

3. PRECIPITATION As the water vapor turns into clouds, rain or snow falls on the side of the mountain near the ocean.

1. EVAPORATION The Sun gives water the energy to become water vapor, a gas.

4. DRY AIR By the time the air passes over the mountain, almost all the water in it is gone.

Differences in air pressure and Earth's rotation create three major belts of planetary winds.

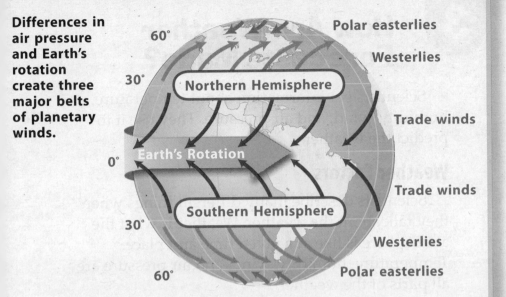

- Polar easterlies
- Westerlies
- Trade winds
- Trade winds
- Westerlies
- Polar easterlies

60°
30°
Northern Hemisphere
0° Earth's Rotation
Southern Hemisphere
30°
60°

Global Wind Patterns

Remember that the uneven heating of Earth makes global pressure belts. Differences in air pressure in these belts make **planetary winds**. Unlike local breezes, planetary winds affect large sections of Earth.

As you can see in the diagram above, three main wind belts cover each hemisphere. These winds do not travel in straight lines. They are made to curve by Earth's rotation.

Another system of global winds can be found in the upper troposphere. These are fast winds called **jet streams**. Winds in these belts can blow as hard as 240 km per hour.

Jet streams and planetary winds affect the weather. Jet streams steer weather from place to place.

CAUSE AND EFFECT

What causes wind?

Summary Wind is caused by differences in air pressure. These differences create both local winds and global winds. List two kinds of global winds.

a. _____

b. _____

 Cause and Effect What causes wind?

Cause		Effect
_____	→	Wind
_____		
_____		
_____		

137

VOCABULARY

air mass a body of air that has about the same temperature and moisture throughout *(noun)*

front the boundary between two air masses *(noun)*

meteorologist a scientist who studies weather *(noun)*

VOCABULARY SKILL: Multiple-Meaning Words

Many words in the English language have more than one meaning. A scientific definition of the word *front* is given above. You probably know another meaning for this word. Write two sentences that use different meanings of the word *front*.

a. _____

_____

b. _____

_____

4.a. Students know that uneven heating of Earth's surface causes air movements.
4.b. Students know that the oceans affect weather.
4.e. Students know that the atmosphere pushes on Earth's surface.

3 How Are Weather Forecasts Made?

Scientists get information about temperature, humidity, wind, and air pressure. They use it to predict the weather.

Weather Factors

Scientists describe many different things when they talk about the weather. Weather is what the atmosphere is like at a given time and place. Temperature, humidity, wind, and air pressure are all parts of the weather.

Temperature measures how hot or cold it is. Humidity is how much water vapor is in the air. Wind, as you know, is moving air. Both wind speed and wind direction can change the weather. And remember that air pressure is the force given off by air.

Clear, sunny weather on Catalina Island

Weather Instruments Weather is measured with tools. A thermometer measures the temperature. It does this in degrees Celsius or Fahrenheit. A rain gauge measures rain.

An anemometer (an uh MAHM uht uhr) measures wind speed. A wind vane is used to figure out wind direction. Air pressure, as you learned, is measured with an instrument called a barometer.

Thermometer

Rain Gauge

Anemometer

Barometer

1. Complete the diagram to tell about weather.

Weather is what the atmosphere is like at a given time and place. Parts of weather are:

2. Circle the picture of the tool that is used to measure wind speed. Put an X on the tool that is used to measure air pressure. Draw a box around the tool that measures temperature.

3. Write the type of air mass next to its description.

Air Mass	Description
	Forms over land where it is cold
	Forms over water where it is warm
	Forms over water where it is cold
	Forms over land where it is warm

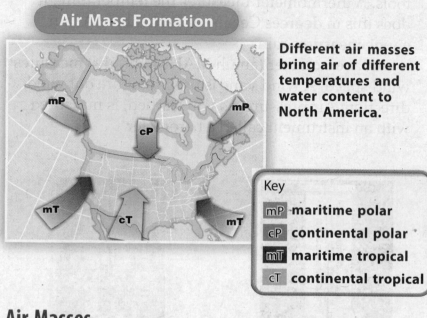

Air Mass Formation

Different air masses bring air of different temperatures and water content to North America.

Key
mP — maritime polar
cP — continental polar
mT — maritime tropical
cT — continental tropical

Air Masses

The troposphere is where almost all weather happens. And, in the troposphere, there are large pockets of air called air masses. An **air mass** is a body of air that has the same temperature and moisture. An air mass is always moving.

The temperature and wetness of an air mass depend on where it began. Polar air masses form where it is cold. Tropical air masses form where it is warm. Continental air masses form over land. They are usually dry. Maritime air masses form over water. They are normally wet.

The map above shows the air masses that affect most of North America. What kind of air mass causes the weather for California? Is it warm or cold? Is it dry or wet? Does this agree with the weather you have where you live?

Fronts

When two air masses meet, a front is formed. A **front** is the boundary between two different kinds of air masses. It is what separates them. If a front is coming, the weather will normally change quickly.

When a warm air mass moves into a place with cold air, a warm front is formed. A warm front normally brings a lot of clouds and rain.

When a cold air mass pushes its way into a warm air mass, you get a cold front. A cold front brings a lot of clouds, heavy rain, and thunderstorms.

Sometimes when two air masses meet, neither one pushes forward. This is a stationary front.

WARM FRONT
A warm front forms when warm air moves into an area. Steady, light rains are common along warm fronts.

COLD FRONT
A cold front forms when cold air moves into an area. Heavy rains often form along a cold front.

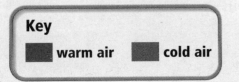

Key

■ warm air   ■ cold air

4. Complete the diagrams to tell about fronts.

Cause	Effect
A warm air mass moves into an area with cold air.	What forms: _____ front Weather: _____ _____

Cause	Effect
A cold air mass moves into an area with warm air.	What forms: _____ front Weather: _____ _____

141

5. (Circle) the warm front on the map.

6. The map shows a front moving through Raleigh, North Carolina.

   a. What kind of front is it?

   _____

   b. What kind of weather would you expect to see there?

   _____

7. Draw a |box| around the cold front on the map.

8. The map shows a front moving through Oklahoma City, Oklahoma.

   a. What kind of front is it?

   _____

   b. What kind of weather would you expect to see there?

   _____

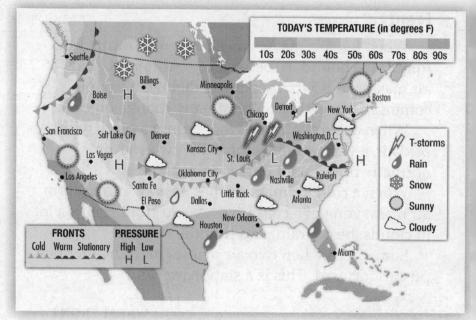

Weather Maps

   Meteorologists (meet ee uhr AHL uh jists) are scientists who study the weather. They watch the weather and collect samples of information, or data. With the help of computers, they make weather maps like the one above. By studying these maps, meteorologists are able to predict, or forecast, future weather.

   Weather maps use symbols. A key is there to help you understand the map. Symbols are used for fronts, as well as cloud cover, precipitation, and pressure.

   Colors are used to show temperatures. In the United States, temperature is usually shown in degrees Fahrenheit.

Weather Radar

Radar is helpful in forecasting weather. A weather radar sends out radio signals. When these signals hit rain or snow, they bounce back and are recorded.

Radar signals can be used to make an image or picture of the storm. You may have seen radar images on television weather reports.

The latest radar technology is a Doppler radar. Doppler not only sees storms, but also figures out how they are moving. This helps track and predict weather, especially thunderstorms and tornadoes.

With the information given by Doppler, meteorologists can warn people about big storms. These early warnings can save lives and property.

THUNDERSTORM
Dense clouds like these are typical of thunderstorms. Meteorologists can identify such clouds on a radar image.

Reno

San Francisco

RADAR
The colors show thunderstorms moving through California and Nevada. Yellow and red show the strongest parts. Green and blue show weaker parts.

9. Complete the diagram to show how weather radar works.

> Radar sends out _____.

> The radio signals hit _____ and bounce back.

> Returning _____ are recorded.

10. Besides seeing storms, what does Doppler radar do?

_____

_____

I Wonder . . . Radar helps meteorologists predict the weather. I wonder how using radar in this way can help people stay safe.

_____

_____

_____

_____

_____

_____

Meteorologists use computers to help them make predictions. Computers help them understand how weather forms and what it will do.

A computer used Doppler radar to make this graph. It shows wind speeds over a 12-hour period.

More Tools for Meteorologists

Today, Doppler radar covers all of the United States and much of the world.

But meteorologists use more than just radar. They still collect data at weather stations all over the world. They compare that data to radar. They also use computers to look at the data and find patterns.

Weather satellites are also important tools. Satellites are machines sent into space to orbit Earth. Weather satellites circle the globe and collect data on weather.

Weather satellites measure cloud temperature, cloud density, water vapor, and land temperature. They can also figure out how much dust or volcanic ash is in the air.

By using all these tools, meteorologists are able to track and predict the weather better than ever. But the atmosphere remains hard to understand.

Short-term forecasts predict the weather for the next day or two. These forecasts are usually correct. But long-term forecasts, which predict the weather more than three days ahead, are not nearly as accurate. They are often wrong.

Doppler radar stations, such as this one in Oklahoma, have become important weather forecasting tools.

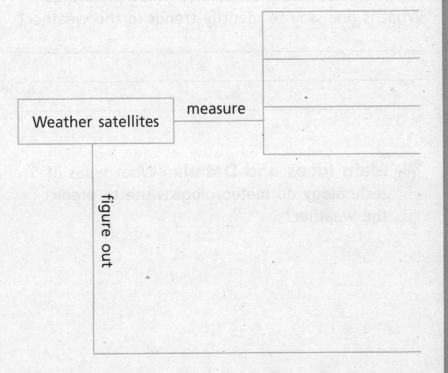

11. Complete the diagram to tell what weather satellites do.

Weather satellites — measure —

figure out

Summary Scientists gather data about temperature, humidity, wind, and air pressure. They use this information to develop weather forecasts. What is one way to identify trends in the weather?

_____

_____

_____

Main Ideas and Details What types of technology do meteorologists use to predict the weather?

```
        ( )              ( )
            \          /
             (         )
              Technology That
              Meteorologists Use
             (         )
            /          \
        ( )              ( )
```

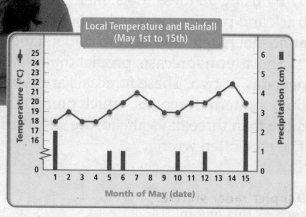

You can use weather instruments to predict the weather. To identify trends in the weather, plot your data in graphs like the one shown here.

Local Temperature and Rainfall (May 1st to 15th)

Be a Weather Expert

You do not have to be a scientist to predict the weather. All you need are the instruments you have read about—a thermometer, a barometer, an anemometer, and a rain gauge. With these tools, you can set up your own weather station.

Use your *Science Notebook* to record weather. You may want to graph the data. Then it is easier to see patterns.

Compare your results with the newspaper, television, or internet. With practice, you will find your results improve.

MAIN IDEA AND DETAILS

What types of technology do meteorologists use to predict the weather?

What Causes Storms?

Severe storms happen in low-pressure systems. In these systems, warm and wet air rises and cools. This forms clouds that bring precipitation.

Thunderstorms

A **thunderstorm** is a storm with lightning, thunder, and heavy rain. It is a common kind of severe weather. Thunderstorms happen most often during warm, humid summers.

Three things must happen in order for there to be a thunderstorm. There must be a lot of moisture in the air. There must be a cold front or a quick heating of the surface; either of these would make air rise quickly. Finally, the rising air must stay warmer than the air around it. When all these things happen, clouds form.

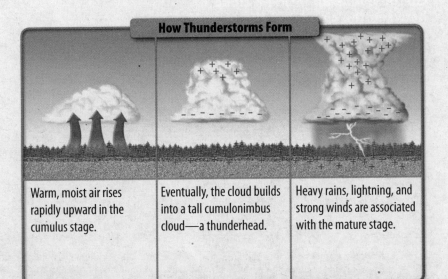

How Thunderstorms Form

Warm, moist air rises rapidly upward in the cumulus stage.

Eventually, the cloud builds into a tall cumulonimbus cloud—a thunderhead.

Heavy rains, lightning, and strong winds are associated with the mature stage.

VOCABULARY

blizzard a snowstorm with strong winds and low temperatures *(noun)*

hurricane a tropical storm with sustained wind speeds near its center of at least 119 km/hr (74 mph) *(noun)*

thunderstorm a storm that delivers lightning, thunder, and heavy rains *(noun)*

tornado a narrow, spinning column of very fast-moving air *(noun)*

VOCABULARY SKILL: Multiple-Meaning Words

In this lesson you will learn about stormy weather. A form of the word *storm* is sometimes used to tell how someone is acting. For example, "Tom's little brother lost his temper and stormed out of the room." Write a definition for *storm* when it is used in this manner.

_____

_____

4.c. Students know what causes severe weather and its effects.

147

1. Complete the diagram to show how a thunderstorm forms.

Step 1, cumulus stage:

_____

_____

↓

Step 2, mature stage:

_____

_____

↓

Step 3, last stage:

_____

_____

2. What is the biggest potential danger brought by severe thunderstorms? Explain.

_____

_____

_____

Thunderstorms often build along cold fronts. The cold air moving at the surface makes warm, wet air rise fast. This is the first part of a thunderstorm, known as the cumulus stage.

The next stage is called the mature stage. In this stage tall, dark clouds form. Heavy rains and strong winds begin. Lightning is also part of the mature stage. Lightning is a powerful electric discharge, or release of energy. We see the discharge as a flash. Lightning heats the air around it, causing a boom of thunder.

In the last stage, the storm loses energy and dies out.

Thunderstorms bring many dangers. But the biggest potential danger brought by severe thunderstorms is from tornadoes. A **tornado** is a thin, spinning column of very fast-moving air.

Lightning occurs when an opposite charge builds up inside a cloud or between the cloud and the ground.

Floods are one of the most common dangers associated with severe weather.

Droughts occur when a high-pressure system stalls over an area for weeks. Ponds and streams may dry up.

Floods and Droughts

A common danger with severe weather is flooding. A flood can form when a river overflows. It can also happen after a short, powerful thunderstorm or a light, steady rain.

The opposite of a flood is a drought. A drought is a long time without any rain. Droughts are common with high-pressure systems. In a high-pressure system, the air sinks. When the air sinks, no precipitation can form.

Droughts kill crops and use up water supplies. Some communities manage droughts by conserving, or saving, water.

---

3. Complete the diagram to compare and contrast floods and droughts.

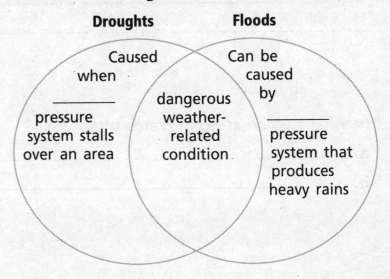

Droughts   Floods

Caused when

_____ pressure system stalls over an area

dangerous weather-related condition

Can be caused by

_____ pressure system that produces heavy rains

4. How can communities help to manage droughts?

_____

_____

5. What is a blizzard?

_____

_____

6. In what two areas do blizzards often occur?

   a. _____

   b. _____

7. List three things that make blizzards dangerous.

   a. _____

   b. _____

   c. _____

Blizzards

In cold regions, thunderstorms do not happen very often in winter, but blizzards do. A **blizzard** is a snowstorm with strong winds and low temperatures. It forms like a thunderstorm, but does not normally have lightning and thunder.

Blizzards happen wherever the winters are cold. They occur in mountainous areas too, such as the Sierra Nevada range in California.

The mix of high winds, cold temperatures, and deep snow make blizzards very dangerous. People can freeze to death if they are caught outside. And because of the deep snow, it can take a community many days to recover from a blizzard.

Blizzards bring high winds, heavy snowfall, and low temperatures.

This photo from space shows the swirling clouds of a hurricane in the Gulf of Mexico.

Hurricanes

Hurricanes are the strongest storms on Earth. They form over warm ocean water. These large, spinning storms have wind speeds at their centers of at least 119 km/hr. The winds of the most powerful hurricanes are twice that strong.

Water vapor is the fuel for hurricanes to form and grow. A hurricane begins as a low-pressure system over warm water. As it gets stronger, thunderstorms begin to spin around the low-pressure zone. As the spinning gets faster, the thunderstorms get bigger.

The warm ocean water offers a big supply of water vapor. So the thunderstorms keep growing, and the spinning gets faster. Hurricanes only begin to weaken when they run into cooler water or land. But making landfall can prove to be catastrophic for cities, states, and even regions of the country.

8. Circle the hurricane in the photo.

9. Where do hurricanes form?

_____

_____

I Wonder . . . Some states are more likely to be hit by a hurricane than others. The states on the southeast Atlantic coast and on the Gulf of Mexico are hit far more often than the states on the northeast coast. Why is this so? What do you think?

_____

_____

_____

_____

10. Put a check mark by each statement that is true about the structure and strength of a hurricane.

_____ Air rises through the eye of the hurricane.

_____ The eye is a calm, low-pressure area.

_____ Air swirls downward just outside the eye.

_____ Rain bands at the edge of the hurricane bring heavy rain.

_____ The strongest hurricanes are classified as category 5.

11. List three hazards of severe weather.

a. _____

b. _____

c. _____

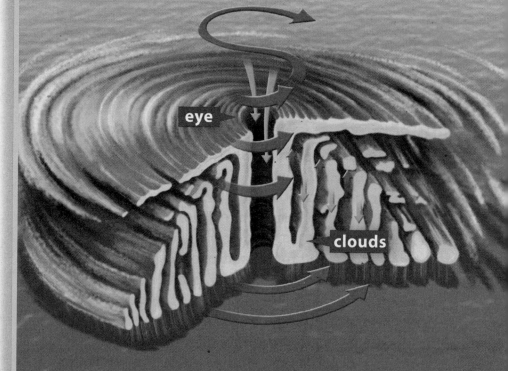

Hurricane Classification		
Strength	Strength	Strength
Category 1	Minimal	74–95 mph
Category 2	Moderate	96–110 mph
Category 3	Extensive	111–130 mph
Category 4	Extreme	131–130 mph
Category 5	Catastrophic	> 155 mph

Warm, moist air

Cooler air

eye

clouds

CROSS SECTION OF A HURRICANE Air sinks through the eye—the calm, low-pressure center of a hurricane. Air swirls upward just outside the eye, forming extremely strong winds. Thick clouds around the eye bring heavy rains, as do rain bands at the edge of the storm.

Heavy rains can cause mudslides such as this one in Laguna Beach, California.

Aftermath!

In early 2005, California got heavy rain and snowfalls. The heavy rain was too much for some of the hillsides. Suddenly, great amounts of mud slid quickly down the hills. In La Conchita, California, a mudslide destroyed 15 homes and killed 10 people.

Mudslides are just one result of severe weather. Hail can destroy crops and damage property. Lightning can start a forest fire. Strong winds from hurricanes and tornadoes can destroy buildings. When an area is hit by severe weather, the damage to life and property can cost billions of dollars.

SEQUENCE

How does a hurricane begin, grow, and then weaken?

Summary Severe storms are associated with low-pressure systems. What kind of weather is associated with high-pressure systems?

_____

Sequence How does a hurricane begin, grow, and then weaken?

> A hurricane begins as a _____ over warm ocean water.

> Thunderstorms begin to spin around the _____. A hurricane forms.

> While the storm is over warm water, the spinning gets faster and the thunderstorms get bigger. The hurricane grows.

> Storm runs into _____. The hurricane weakens.

153

Circle the terms on this page that describe types of storms.

air mass a body of air that has about the same temperature and moisture throughout

masa de aire cuerpo de aire cuya temperatura y humedad es prácticamente homogénea

air pressure the force exerted by air in all directions on a given area

presión atmosférica fuerza que el aire ejerce en todas direcciones en una zona determinada

atmosphere a mixture of gases that surround a planet

atmósfera capa gaseosa que rodea un planeta

blizzard a snowstorm with strong winds and low temperatures

ventisca tormenta de nieve con fuertes vientos y bajas temperatures

front the boundary between two air masses

frente el límite entre dos masas de aire

hurricane a tropical storm with sustained wind speeds near its center of at least 119 km/hr (74 mph)

huracán tormenta tropical con vientos cuyas velocidades cerca de su centro son de al menos 119 km/h (74 mph)

Glossary

jet stream narrow belt of high-speed winds in the upper troposphere

   corriente de aire círculo estrecho de vientos a alta velocidad en la capa superior de la troposfera

land breeze a local wind that blows at night from land toward water

   viento terral viento local que sopla de noche desde la tierra hasta el agua

meteorologist a scientist who studies weather

   meteorólogo científico que estudia el tiempo atmosférico

mountain breeze a local wind that flows downhill and is produced by cooler, denser air above the mountain slopes

   brisa de montaña viento local producido por aire más frío y denso que se desliza por las pendientes de las montañas

planetary winds long-lasting wind patterns that cover a large area of Earth

   vientos planetarios patrones duraderos de vientos que cubren un área grande de la Tierra

sea breeze a local wind that blows from water toward land during the day

   brisa marina viento local que sopla desde el mar hacia la tierra durante el día

Circle the terms on this page that are associated with moving air.

Visit www.eduplace.com to play puzzles and word games.

Circle the term on this page that is the same in both Spanish and English.

Glossary

thunderstorm a storm that delivers lightning, thunder, and heavy rains

tormenta perturbación atmosférica acompañada de fuertes lluvias, truenos y relámpagos

tornado a narrow, spinning column of very fast-moving air

tornado columna estrecha de aire que se mueve muy rápidamente en círculos

valley breeze a local wind produced by the movement of cooler air from the valley that moves up a mountain slope

brisa del valle viento local producido por el movimiento de aire más frío del valle, que se mueve montaña arriba

weather what the atmosphere is like at a given time and place

tiempo condiciones climatológicas de la atmósfera en una hora y lugar determinado

Think About What You Have Read

Vocabulary

❶ The boundary between two air masses of different properties is a/an _____.

A) tornado

B) front

C) air pressure

D) sea breeze

Comprehension

❷ The most powerful type of a storm is a/an _____.

❸ A sea breeze happens when air moves _____.

❹ How can mudslides form?

Critical Thinking

❺ Which is more reliable—a short-term weather forecast or a long-term weather forecast for your area? Explain.

K W L

WHAT DID YOU LEARN?

Vocabulary

❶ Circle the correct answer on the page.

Comprehension

❷ _____

❸ _____
_____

❹ _____
_____

❺ _____
_____
_____
_____

KWL

WHAT DO YOU KNOW?

Tell one fact that you know about each of these parts of the solar system:

a. Sun _____

_____

_____

b. Planets _____

_____

_____

c. Moons _____

_____

_____

d. Asteroids, comets, and meteors _____

_____

_____

The Solar System

Contents

KWL

WHAT DO YOU WANT TO KNOW?

Skim the pictures and headings in this chapter. List one thing that you want to find out about each of these parts of the solar system.

a. The Sun _____

_____

b. Planets _____

_____

c. Moons _____

_____

d. Asteroids, comets, and meteors _____

_____

_____

VOCABULARY

nuclear fusion the process in which the nuclei of atoms fuse together to form a larger nucleus *(noun)*

sunspot a dark-appearing area on the Sun that is cooler than surrounding areas *(noun)*

VOCABULARY SKILL: Compound Words

Compound words are made of two words that are joined together. The word *sunspot* is made of the words *sun* and *spot*. Draw a picture of what you think a sunspot looks like. Label the Sun and the sunspot on your drawing.

1

What Is Earth's Sun Like?

The Sun is the largest thing in the solar system. It gives us most of the energy we need to live.

An Average Star

The Sun is the closest star to Earth. It is a yellow star. It is not the biggest star. It is not the hottest or coolest star. Compared to other stars, the Sun is average-sized.

The Sun is a giant ball of hot, glowing gas called plasma. It is 150 million km from Earth. The Sun is about 4.6 billion years old, and it is so big that more than 1,000,000 Earths could fit inside it!

The Sun is the most important thing in the solar system. Its gravitational pull is the force that keeps Earth and all of the other planets in orbit. Earth gets its energy from the Sun. Life on our planet could not exist without the Sun.

The Sun is a constant source of both light and heat.

Sun Statistics	
Diameter	1,390,000 km
Mass	2×10^{27} metric tons
Surface Temperature	5,500°C
Core Temperature	15,000,000°C
Composition	74% hydrogen 24% helium 2% other elements
Age	4.6 billion years

160

5.a. Students know some characteristics of the Sun and that the Sun is the center of the solar system.

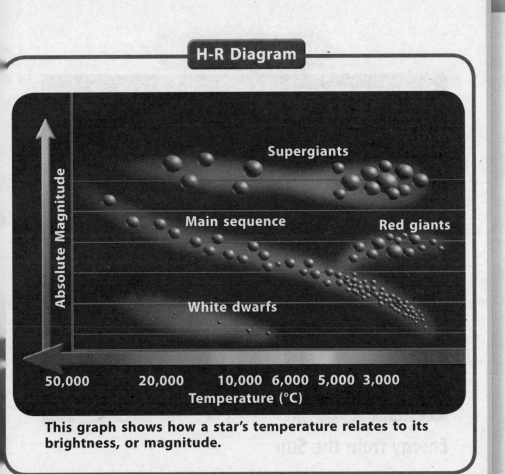

H-R Diagram

Supergiants

Main sequence

Red giants

White dwarfs

Absolute Magnitude

50,000   20,000   10,000 6,000 5,000 3,000
Temperature (°C)

This graph shows how a star's temperature relates to its brightness, or magnitude.

Sunspots are dark places on the Sun's surface. They look dark because they are cooler than the places around them. The number of sunspots increases and decreases in an eleven-year cycle.

Solar flares shoot particles, or small pieces of the Sun, into space. These particles reach Earth and upset radio signals. They also cause auroras. Auroras are colorful lights that can be seen near the North and South Poles.

1. Circle the Sun's surface temperature in the "Sun Statistics" table. What is the temperature of the surface of the Sun?

_____

2. On the horizontal axis of the H-R diagram, star colors go from red on the right to blue on the left. Circle the part of the horizontal axis that represents yellow stars. What is the temperature range of yellow stars?

_____

3. What part of the horizontal axis represents stars like our Sun?

_____

4. What can you conclude about the temperature of sunspots?

_____

_____

5. (Circle) the Sun's core.

6. Put a check mark next to each statement that is true about the Sun.

_____ The Sun is denser than Earth.

_____ The Sun is made mostly of hydrogen and helium.

_____ The Sun's energy comes from nuclear fusion.

_____ Nuclear fusion takes place mainly at the Sun's surface.

_____ Nuclear fusion changes hydrogen to helium.

7. (Circle) the nebula in the diagram on page 163. What is a nebula?

_____

_____

8. The Sun is a main-sequence star. (Circle) the next stage in the Sun's life cycle.

Structure of the Sun

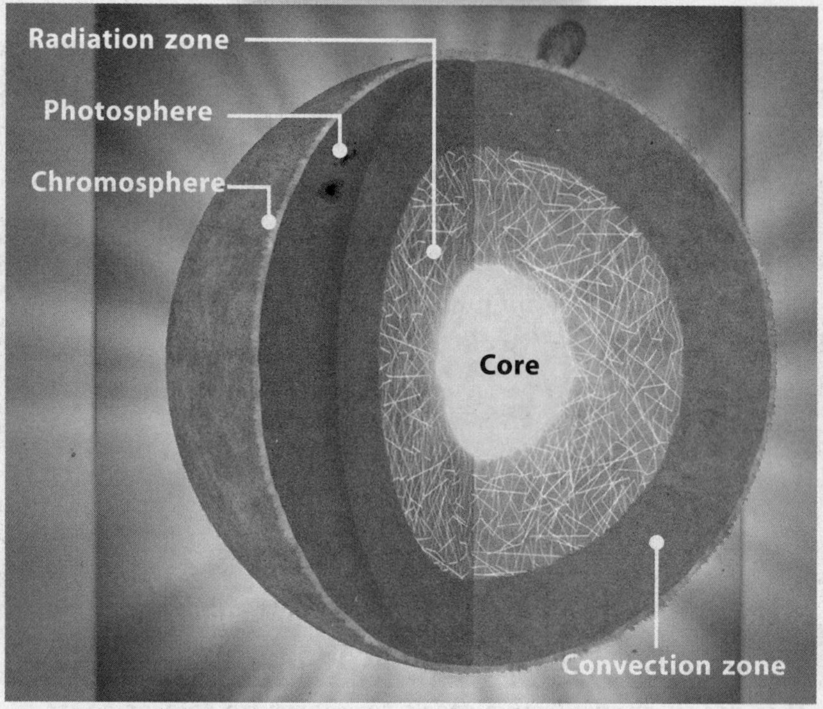

Radiation zone
Photosphere
Chromosphere
Core
Convection zone

Energy from the Sun

The Sun is made mostly of the gases hydrogen and helium. These elements are very light. Even though the Sun is the biggest body in our solar system, it is only a quarter as dense as Earth.

The Sun is very hot. At the core, the part deepest inside the Sun, the temperature is 15,000,000°C. It is in the core that the Sun's energy is released.

Nuclear fusion is how all stars, including the Sun, release energy. Within stars a gas called hydrogen changes into helium. This change happens in the very smallest of places—inside atoms. But fusion is capable of releasing extremely large amounts of energy.

Life Cycle of Stars

Scientists use life cycles to describe stars. A star's life has a beginning, a middle, and an end.

Stars come from huge spinning clouds of dust and gas. This cloud is called a *nebula* (NEB yuh luh). The nebula gets more and more dense as gravity pulls it together. It gets hot and it starts to glow. Fusion begins. A star is born.

A star's life will last billions of years. But some day it will run out of fuel. That is when a star dies.

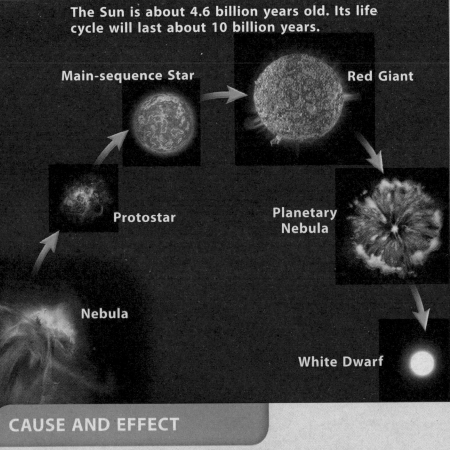

The Sun is about 4.6 billion years old. Its life cycle will last about 10 billion years.

Main-sequence Star

Red Giant

Protostar

Planetary Nebula

Nebula

White Dwarf

CAUSE AND EFFECT

What causes a nebula to collapse into a dense mass?

Summary The Sun is the largest body in the solar system. Earth gets its energy from the Sun. The Sun's energy comes from nuclear fusion. It is an average-sized star that is about halfway through its life cycle.

List three more facts about the Sun.

a. _____

_____

b. _____

_____

c. _____

_____

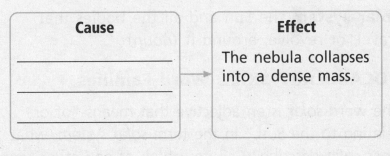

Cause and Effect What causes a nebula to collapse into a dense mass?

Cause	Effect
_____ _____ _____	The nebula collapses into a dense mass.

VOCABULARY

asteroid a relatively small, rocky object that orbits the Sun *(noun)*

comet a small, orbiting body made of dust, ice, and frozen gases *(noun)*

galaxy a huge system of gas, dust, and stars *(noun)*

meteor a chunk of matter that enters Earth's atmosphere and is heated by friction with the air *(noun)*

meteoroid a bit of rock or metal that orbits the Sun *(noun)*

planet a large body that revolves around the Sun *(noun)*

solar system the Sun and all the bodies that travel, or revolve, around it *(noun)*

VOCABULARY SKILL: Word Families

The word *solar* is an adjective that means "of or relating to the Sun." In the term *solar system*, what does *solar* describe? Can you think of any other terms that use the word *solar*?

_____

_____

5.a. Students know some characteristics of the Sun and that the Sun is the center of the solar system.
5.b. Students know what makes up the solar system.

2 What Orbits the Sun?

The Sun and the planets make up the solar system. The solar system is a small part of the Milky Way galaxy.

The Sun and Its Neighbors

Earth's neighborhood is the solar system. The **solar system** is the Sun and all the things that orbit, or revolve, around it. Earth is one of the planets. **Planets** are large bodies that revolve around a star.

The Sun is the biggest thing in the solar system. Its gravity holds everything together. Bodies smaller than planets help make up the solar system, too. There are moons, comets, asteroids, and meteoroids.

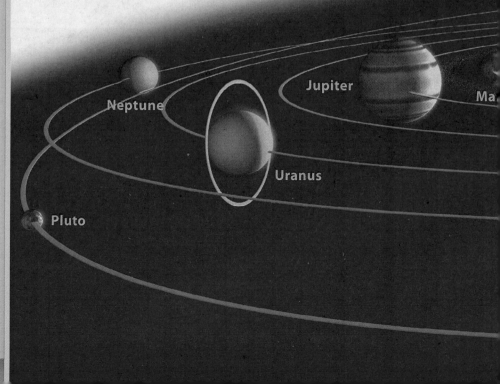

Neptune

Jupiter

Ma...

Uranus

Pluto

The solar system is just a small part of the Milky Way galaxy. A **galaxy** (GAL uhk see) is a huge system of gas, dust, and stars.

Our solar system began as a hot spinning cloud of gases and dust. The Sun formed in the hot center of the cloud. Matter in the cooler part of the cloud came together to make the planets and their moons.

The planets follow a path, or orbit, around the Sun. It is the Sun's gravity that holds all the planets in their orbits.

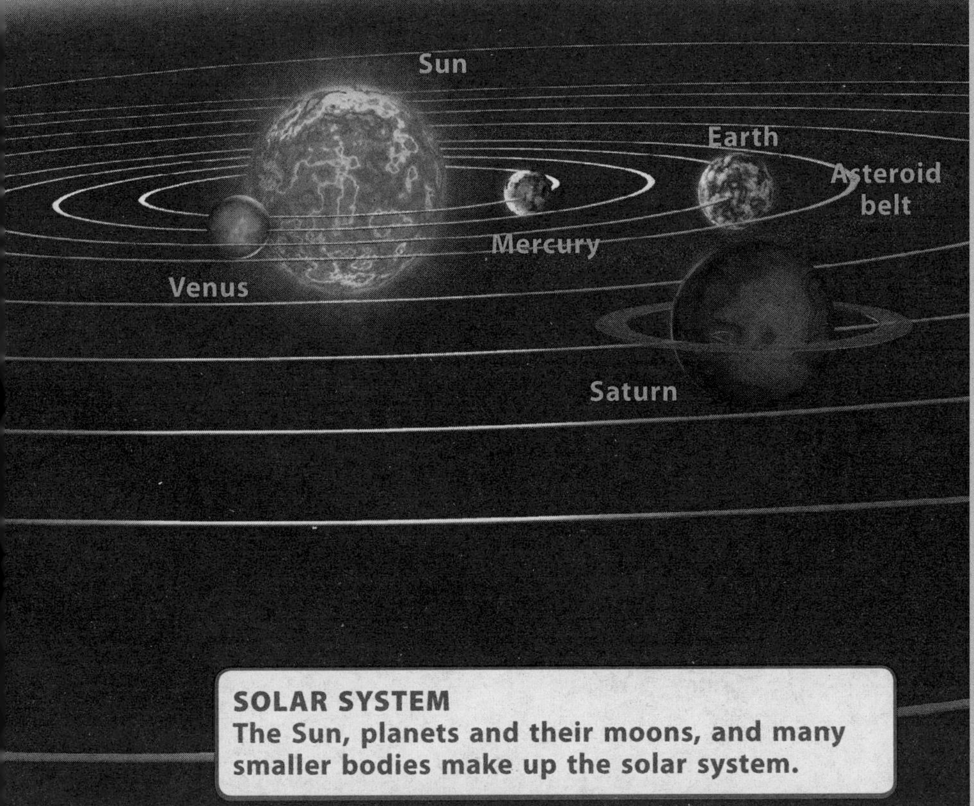

SOLAR SYSTEM
The Sun, planets and their moons, and many smaller bodies make up the solar system.

1. Write the correct term next to its description.

Term	Description
_____	large bodies that revolve around a star
_____	the Sun and everything that orbits it
_____	a huge system of gas, dust, and stars

2. How is the solar system different from the Milky Way galaxy?

_____

_____

_____

3. Complete the outline about moons.

  I. A moon is a natural _____.

    A. Moons orbit _____.

    B. More than _____ moons are in the solar system.

    C. Many moons have the same features as _____.

  II. Earth's moon is often called _____.

    A. American astronauts last _____ _____ in 1972.

    B. We learned about the Moon from _____ brought back by the astronauts.

Moons

A moon is a natural satellite. A satellite circles, or orbits, a planet. Earth's moon is often just called *the* Moon. It is a quarter the size of Earth.

A lot of what we know about the Moon comes from trips people took there. Between 1969 and 1972, American astronauts were part of missions that landed on the Moon. The astronauts gathered moon rocks and studied the Moon's surface.

Astronaut Dave Scott planted the U.S. flag on the Moon. *Astronaut* means "star voyager."

Asteroids are small, rocky bodies that orbit the Sun. Many of these asteroids lie in a belt between Mars and Jupiter.

Other planets also have moons. In fact, scientists have found more than 140 other moons in the solar system. Many moons have the same features as planets.

Asteroids

An **asteroid** (AS tuh royd) is a small, rocky object that orbits the Sun. Scientists think there are millions of asteroids in the solar system. Most orbit the Sun in an area called the asteroid belt. This belt is between Mars and Jupiter.

4. Complete this diagram to compare moons and asteroids.

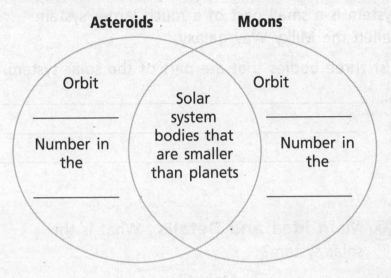

5. Most asteroids are in the asteroid belt. Between which two planets is the asteroid belt?

_____

Summary   The Sun and the bodies that revolve around it make up the solar system. The solar system is a small part of a much larger system called the Milky Way galaxy.

List three bodies that are part of the solar system.

a. _____

b. _____

c. _____

Main Idea and Details   What is the solar system?

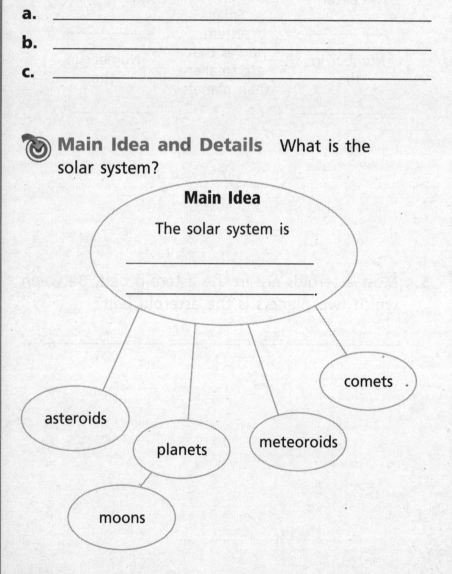

Main Idea

The solar system is

_____

_____ .

asteroids

planets

moons

meteoroids

comets

Comet Hyakutake

Named for its discoverer, Yuji Hyakutake, this comet was one of the brightest to approach the Sun in the 20th century.

Comets and Meteors

A **comet** is a small body of dust, ice, and frozen gases. All comets orbit the Sun. Comets have a glowing tail that gets longer as it nears the Sun. These tails can be millions of kilometers long!

The orbits of some comets take them around the Sun in less than 200 years. These are called short-period comets. Others can take up to 30 million years to orbit the Sun! They are called long-period comets.

A **meteor** is a chunk of matter that enters Earth's atmosphere. These chunks are heated in the atmosphere, and they burn as they fall.

A few meteors are very large—as big as asteroids. But most are as small as a grain of sand. Meteors begin as **meteoroids**, which are bits of rock or metal that orbit the Sun.

MAIN IDEA AND DETAILS

What is the solar system?

What Are the Planets Like?

The four planets closest to the Sun are the inner planets. The other four planets are the outer planets.

Discovering the Solar System

People used to think Earth was the center of the solar system. They thought everything orbited around it. This is called the geocentric model. People thought it was true for over 2,000 years.

Using a telescope, Galileo made many important discoveries about the planets and their moons.

VOCABULARY

inner planet any of the first four planets (Mercury, Venus, Earth, and Mars) from the Sun (noun)

outer planet any of the planets farthest from the Sun (Jupiter, Saturn, Uranus, and Neptune) (noun)

VOCABULARY SKILL: Prefix/Suffix

In this lesson you will see the words *geocentric* and *heliocentric*. The prefix *geo-* comes from a Greek word meaning "Earth." *Helio-* comes from a Greek word meaning "Sun." The word part *-centric* comes from a Latin word meaning "the center of a circle." The suffix *-ic* makes certain words into adjectives. Use this information to write definitions for *geocentric* and *heliocentric*.

_____

_____

5.b. Students know what makes up the solar system.

1. (Circle) the telescopes. What is a telescope?

_____

_____

2. What is an astronomer?

_____

_____

3. Write the name of the astronomer next to what he is known for.

Astronomer	Known For
_____	Reasoning that the Sun is at the center of the solar system
_____	Being the first person to use a telescope

In 1542, a scientist named Copernicus found that the Sun was the center of the solar system. Earth, he reasoned, was just one of the planets that orbit the Sun. This is called the heliocentric model. We now know this is correct.

In 1610, a man named Galileo was the first person to use a telescope. Today, astronomers still use telescopes. Astronomers are scientists who study space. Some of the best telescopes are built on top of mountains or sent into space. Astronomers put telescopes in these places so that they get the clearest views of outer space.

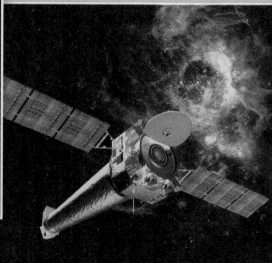

Some telescopes are sent into space to get clearer pictures.

The Inner Planets

The first four planets from the Sun are Mercury, Venus, Earth, and Mars. These are called the **inner planets** because they are closest to the Sun. The inner planets are rocky and small.

Mercury is the smallest inner planet. Mercury is very hot in the day and very cold at night. It has a thin atmosphere and its surface is covered with craters. Craters are holes in the ground left after asteroids or other space objects hit the surface.

MERCURY There are many craters on Mercury.

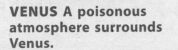

VENUS A poisonous atmosphere surrounds Venus.

4. List the inner planets.

a. _____

b. _____

c. _____

d. _____

5. Complete the diagram to tell about the planet Mercury.

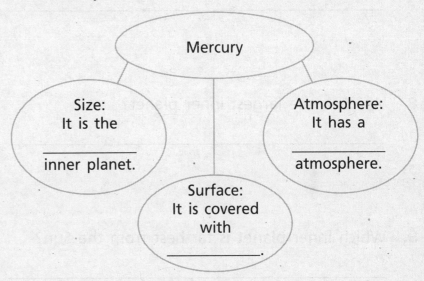

Mercury

Size:
It is the
_____
inner planet.

Atmosphere:
It has a
_____
atmosphere.

Surface:
It is covered
with
_____.

171

6. List four facts about Venus.

a. _____

b. _____

c. _____

d _____

7. Which planet is almost the same size as Earth?

_____

8. Which is the largest inner planet?

_____

9. Which inner planet is farthest from the Sun?

_____

Venus is the second planet from the Sun. It is covered by thick, poisonous clouds. The temperature is hot enough to melt metal, and the pressure would crush your bones.

You are familiar with Earth. It is the only planet known to have water and life.

Mars is about half the size of Earth. Mars's surface looks as if it may have once had water. Its surface is mostly flat, but it does have canyons and volcanoes.

Inner Planets		
Planet	Diameter (km)	Distance from Sun (million km)
Mercury	4,880	57.9
Venus	12,100	108.2
Earth	12,758	149.6
Mars	6,800	227.9

MARS Like Earth, Mars has ice caps at both poles.

EARTH Earth's temperature and its atmosphere make it the only planet in the solar system known to support life.

The Outer Planets

The **outer planets** are Jupiter, Saturn, Uranus, and Neptune. These planets are all very big and made mostly of gas.

Jupiter is the biggest planet in our solar system. It is the fifth planet from the Sun. It is known for its storms, including one so large that it is called the Great Red Spot. Jupiter has rings and many moons.

The planet famous for its rings is Saturn. Saturn is the sixth planet from the Sun. Its rings are made mostly of ice. Saturn is also the least dense of all the planets. In fact, if you could put Saturn in a giant tub of water, it would float!

Outer Planets		
Planet	**Diameter (km)**	**Distance from Sun (million km)**
Jupiter	142,800	778
Saturn	12,000	1,427
Uranus	50,800	2,870
Neptune	48,600	4,500

JUPITER Jupiter is the biggest planet in the solar system. It has more than 60 moons.

SATURN Saturn is surrounded by rings made of thousands of particles.

10. List the outer planets.

a. _____

b. _____

c. _____

d. _____

11. Write the name of the outer planet next to its description.

Outer Planet	Description
_____	has a Great Red Spot
_____	famous for its rings
_____	biggest planet in the solar system
_____	least dense of all the planets
_____	farthest from the Sun

12. Put a check mark next to each statement that is true about Neptune.

_____ Neptune is rocky and cold.

_____ Neptune has the fastest winds in the solar system.

_____ Neptune is the seventh planet from the Sun.

13. Complete the diagram to compare Uranus and Pluto.

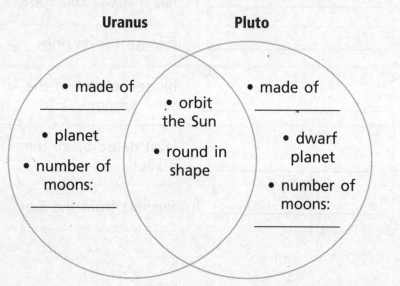

Uranus   **Pluto**

- made of
  _____
- planet
- number of moons:
  _____

- orbit the Sun
- round in shape

- made of
  _____
- dwarf planet
- number of moons:
  _____

Uranus is the seventh planet from the Sun. Uranus is made mostly of gas. It has 27 moons and 11 rings.

Neptune has the fastest winds in the solar system, with speeds almost 20 times faster than a hurricane! Neptune has 13 moons.

Pluto was once known as the ninth planet. Today it is known as a dwarf planet. Dwarf planets are small, round objects that orbit the Sun. Pluto is rocky and cold. It has three moons.

URANUS Some of the gas on Uranus gives it a greenish color.

NEPTUNE Neptune and its largest moon may collide in the next 100 million years.

PLUTO Pluto is a dwarf planet. It has ice caps at its poles.

The space shuttle takes off attached to a rocket. To return to Earth, it lands like an airplane.

Exploring Space

Astronomers count on spacecraft to learn more about the universe. The space shuttle is a vehicle that takes people into space. Tests are made as it orbits Earth. The space shuttle can be used over and over.

A space probe is a spacecraft that carries special equipment. Some probes visit distant planets and moons to help us learn new things. Sometimes probes carry robots to a planet to collect material. Two robots recently explored Mars.

COMPARE AND CONTRAST

How are Venus and Earth similar and different?

Summary The four planets closest to the Sun are called the inner planets. The remaining four planets are the outer planets.

List three methods for learning more about the universe.

a. _____

b. _____

c. _____

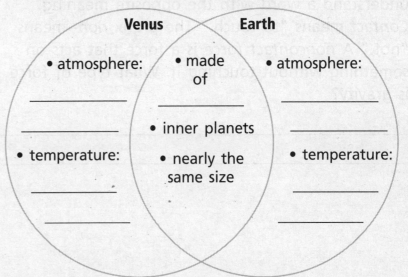

Compare and Contrast How are Venus and Earth similar and different?

Venus — Earth

- atmosphere: _____ • made of _____ • atmosphere: _____

_____ • inner planets _____

- temperature: _____ • nearly the same size • temperature: _____

_____ _____

175

VOCABULARY

gravity the gravitational attraction of Earth, or any massive body in space, on objects at or near its surface. *(noun)*

VOCABULARY SKILL: Antonyms and Synonyms

You can use your knowledge of a familiar word to understand a word with the opposite meaning. *Contact* means "to touch." The prefix *non-* means "not." A *noncontact force* is a force that acts on something without touching it. What type of force is gravity?

_____

_____

4 What Keeps Planets in Their Orbits?

The path of a planet around the Sun is caused by gravity.

Gravitation

The force that causes objects to fall to Earth is called gravitation. Gravitation is the pull of any two objects toward each other. Every object in the universe pulls on every other object.

The gravitational pull between Earth and objects near its surface is called **gravity**. The term *gravity* can be used for all bodies in space.

The Force of Gravitation

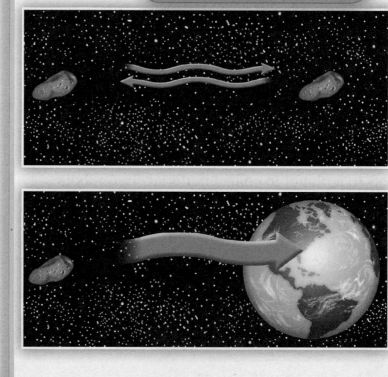

Left alone in space, two large rocks would gravitate toward each other.

Near Earth, however, objects with small mass fall toward Earth without Earth moving toward them.

5.c. Students know that gravity holds the planets in orbit around the Sun.

The strength of gravity depends on the size of the objects and their distance from each other. For example, if the Sun were twice as big, the gravitational force on Earth would be twice as strong. If Earth were closer to the Sun, the pull also would be stronger.

Gravity is a weak force unless the objects are very large. If you hold two pencils nearby, they will pull toward each other. But you do not feel it because they are so small. Now drop them. They both fall to the floor. They do so because they are pulled by the huge mass of Earth. Earth pulls on the pencils much harder than they pull on each other.

When you drop two objects, they go toward the ground and not each other.

1. What is gravitation?

_____

_____

2. Complete the diagram to tell about gravitational force.

The strength of gravity depends on

3. Complete the diagram to show how the nebula that formed our solar system collapsed.

Cause		Effect
_____ _____	→	The nebula collapses forming a star and planets.

I Wonder . . . Earth, an inner planet, is small, dense, and made of rock. Jupiter, an outer planet, is is made of gases that are light elements. Yet Jupiter has more than 300 times more mass than Earth does. How is this possible?

_____

_____

_____

_____

Formation of the Solar System

Gravity helped make our solar system. The force of gravity collapsed the cloud of gas and dust, called a nebula, into a star and planets.

The inner planets became dense and rocky because where they formed was very hot. All of the light elements were changed to a gas, or vaporized away.

The outer planets formed where it was cool. They were made of ice, gas, and dust. The temperature was right for them to become gas giants.

Over billions of years, the force of gravity collapsed a nebula into the solar system.

Planet Orbitals

The closer a planet is to the Sun, the faster it moves. As a result, the inner planets travel faster in their orbits than the outer planets. Since the outer planets move slower and have a greater distance to cover, they take much longer to orbit the Sun. The dwarf planet Pluto is forty times more distant from the Sun than Earth is. Pluto moves so slowly that it takes 248 Earth years to orbit the Sun.

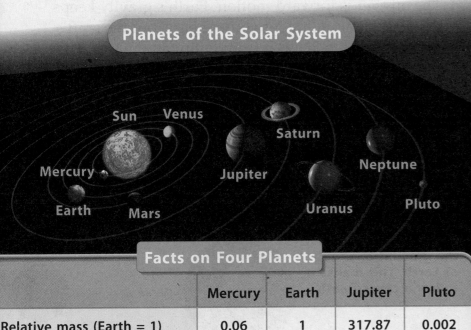

Planets of the Solar System

Sun Venus Saturn Mercury Jupiter Neptune Earth Mars Uranus Pluto

Facts on Four Planets

	Mercury	Earth	Jupiter	Pluto
Relative mass (Earth = 1)	0.06	1	317.87	0.002
Average distance to Sun (millions of km)	58	150	778	5900
Average orbital speed (km/s)	47.5	29.8	13.1	4.7
Orbital period	88 Days	365 Days	12 Years	248 Years

4. Circle the inner planets.

5. Which planet is moving fastest in its orbit?

   _____

6. Draw a box around Jupiter. Jupiter is the largest planet in the solar system. Its orbital speed, however, is neither the fastest nor the slowest among the planets. Why is this so?

   _____

   _____

Summary Gravitation is the pull of any two objects toward each other. The path followed by a planet around the Sun is caused by the gravitational attraction between the Sun and the planet.

What keeps the planets from being pulled into the Sun?

_____

_____

_____

🎯 **Draw Conclusions** Why are the inner planets not made of light elements?

Text Clue	Prior Knowledge	Conclusion
Inner planets formed near the Sun, where it was hottest.	Heat can vaporize, or change to gas, lighter elements.	_____ _____ _____ _____ _____ _____

Weightlessness

Weightlessness is the feeling of being lighter than a feather. If you are falling and your surroundings are falling at the same rate, then you will experience weightlessness.

In a spacecraft orbiting Earth, all of the astronauts are in a state of free-fall. They and their ship are all falling at the same rate. As the astronauts and their ship fall toward Earth at the same speed, they seem to float.

But why doesn't the spacecraft fall to Earth then? The answer is forward motion. Earth's gravity keeps the craft from sailing into outer space, but the craft's forward motion keeps it from falling into Earth. This is the same reason why the Moon isn't sucked into Earth by its gravity. It is also why all of the planets do not go crashing into the Sun.

The Moon is affected by two forces. It has both its forward motion and the gravitational pull of Earth. This makes it follow a curved path.

DRAW CONCLUSIONS

Why are the inner planets not made of light elements?

asteroid (AS tuh royd) a relatively small, rocky object that orbits the Sun

   asteroide objeto rocoso relativamente pequeño que orbita alrededor del Sol

comet a small, orbiting body made of dust, ice, and frozen gases

   cometa pequeño cuerpo celeste orbital compuesto de polvo, hielo y gases helados

galaxy (GAL uhk see) a huge system of gas, dust, and stars

   galaxia gigantesco sistema de gas, compuesto de polvo y estrellas

gravity the gravitational attraction of Earth, or any massive body in space, on objects at or near its surface

   gravedad atracción gravitacional de la Tiera o cualquier cuerpo gigantesco en el espacio sobre los objetos que están cerca o sobre su superficie

inner planet any of the first four planets (Mercury, Venus, Earth, and Mars) from the Sun

   planetas interiores cualquiera de los cuatro planetas más cercanos al Sol (Mercurio, Venus, Tierra y Marte)

meteor a chunk of matter that enters Earth's atmosphere and is heated by friction with the air

   meteoro pedazo de materia que entra en la atmósfera terrestre y se calienta por la fricción con el aire

(Circle) all the words on this page that describe space bodies found in our solar system.

Visit www.eduplace.com to play puzzles and word games.

The English and the Spanish are very similar for most of the terms on this page. (Circle) a term that is very different in Spanish and in English.

Glossary

meteoroid a bit of rock or metal that orbits the Sun

  meteorito trozo de roca o de metal que gira alrededor del Sol

nuclear fusion the process in which the nuclei of atoms fuse together to form a larger nucleus

  fusión nuclear proceso mediante el cual los núcleos de los átomos se funden para formar un núcleo mayor

outer planet any of the planets farthest from the Sun (Jupiter, Saturn, Uranus, and Neptune)

  planeta exterior cualquiera de los planetas más alejados del Sol (Júpiter, Saturno, Urano y Neptuno)

planet a large body that revolves around the Sun

  planeta gran cuerpo estelar que gira alrededor del Sol

solar system the Sun and all the bodies that travel, or revolve, around it

  sistema solar el Sol y todos los cuerpos que se mueven, o giran, a su alrededor

sunspot a dark-appearing area on the Sun that is cooler than surrounding areas

  mancha solar zona oscura del Sol que es más fría que las zonas que la rodean

Think About What You Have Read

Vocabulary

❶ Stars produce energy by _____.

A) gravity

B) comets

C) outer planets.

D) nuclear fusion

Comprehension

❷ Dark, cool areas on the surface of the Sun are called _____.

❸ Objects in the solar system are held in their orbits by the gravitational pull of _____.

❹ What do the outer planets have in common?

Critical Thinking

❺ What is another way you might divide the planets into two groups other than the inner planets and the outer planets?

KWL

WHAT DID YOU LEARN?

Vocabulary

❶ Circle the correct answer on the page.

Comprehension

❷ _____

❸ _____

_____

❹ _____

_____

Critical Thinking

❺ _____

_____

_____

_____

183

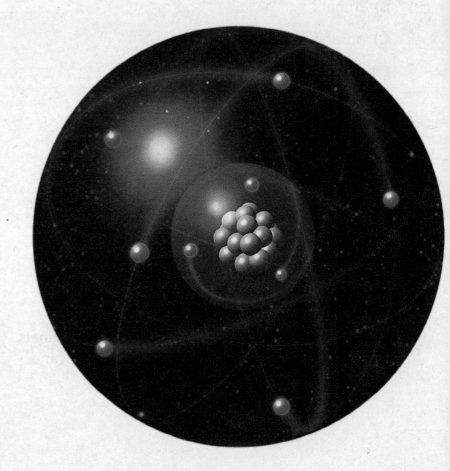

Atoms and Elements

KWL

WHAT DO YOU KNOW?

Write or draw something that you know about atoms.

_____

_____

Tell something that you know about elements.

_____

_____

What do you know about the periodic table?

_____

_____

Contents

WHAT DO YOU WANT TO KNOW?

Read all the headings in this chapter. List one thing you want to find out about each of these topics:

a. Atoms _____
_____
_____

b. Elements _____
_____
_____

c. The periodic table _____
_____
_____

VOCABULARY SKILL: Word Origins

The word *neutron* is based on the Latin word *neuter*, which means "neither." How can this information help you remember the meaning of *neutron*?

1.b. Students know that matter is made of atoms. Atoms may combine to form molecules.
1.e. Students know that instruments show that atoms and molecules often occur in patterns.

1 What Are Atoms and Elements?

All matter is made of atoms. Atoms are the smallest units of elements.

Matter

Matter is anything that has mass and takes up space. It is all the "stuff" in the universe.

All matter is made of elements. An **element** is a substance that cannot be broken down any further. Water is not an element. But hydrogen and oxygen, the two gases that join to make water, are elements. Elements are made of only one kind of atom. An **atom** is the smallest particle of an element that still has the properties of that element. Atoms are the tiny building blocks of matter.

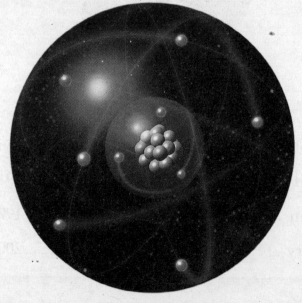

An atom is the smallest particle of an element that still has the properties of that element.

Atoms have a nucleus surrounded by moving electrons. The **nucleus** (NOO klee uhs) is the structure at the center of an atom. A nucleus has two kinds of particles: protons and neutrons. A **proton** is a small, positively charged particle. A **neutron** is a particle that has no charge.

The nucleus contains almost all the mass of the atom even though it takes up very little space. The rest of the atom is mostly empty space through which electrons move. **Electrons** are negatively charged particles.

There are an equal number of protons and electrons in every atom. The number of neutrons can be different.

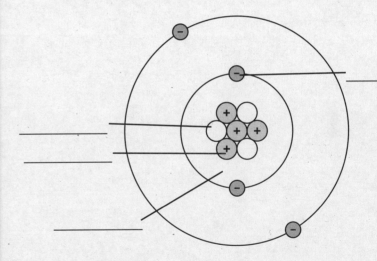

Nucleus

Electron

What if an atom's nucleus were enlarged to the size of a quarter? If so, an atom centered on the pitcher's mound would reach to the warning track!

1. Complete the sentences about atoms and elements.

   a. All matter is made up of _____.

   b. Elements are made up of only _____ _____.

   c. An atom is the _____ of an element.

2. Complete the diagram by labeling the parts of an atom.

187

3. How many of the over 100 elements are common?

_____

4. List three examples of ways carbon atoms group together to form different kinds of matter.

a. _____

b. _____

c. _____

Organization of Atoms

There are more than 100 elements, but only about 50 are common. So how are there so many different kinds of matter around you? The answer comes from how atoms join together.

The element carbon gives a good example. One way carbon atoms join is as coal. Coal is a hard black substance used as fuel. Another way carbon atoms group is as graphite. Graphite is gray or black and feels slippery. It is found in pencil lead. Diamonds are another form of pure carbon. They are the hardest substance found on Earth.

So, even though carbon is only one element, the way its atoms can join makes many different kinds of matter.

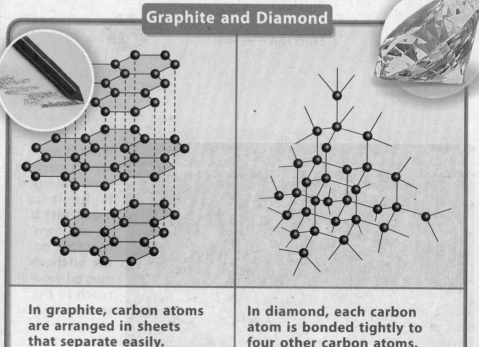

Graphite and Diamond

In graphite, carbon atoms are arranged in sheets that separate easily.

In diamond, each carbon atom is bonded tightly to four other carbon atoms.

Elements Alone and Joined

An element's properties come from the atoms that make it up. Some properties are ability to conduct electricity, hardness, and density. What are some of the properties of the elements shown here?

Some elements are found alone. But most elements make compounds. A **compound** is a substance made of two or more elements that are chemically joined.

The paper and ink in this book are compounds. Salt and sugar are too. Chemical compounds are everywhere!

Aluminum is a metallic element that is strong but lightweight.

The helium in these balloons is less dense than air, so they float.

Copper can be stretched into wires. It also conducts electricity well.

Silver is a shiny metal that is soft enough to be formed into jewelry.

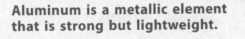

5. List three properties of elements.

   a. _____

   b. _____

   c. _____

6. What is a compound?

   _____

   _____

   _____

189

Summary All matter is made up of particles called atoms. Atoms have a nucleus made up of protons and neutrons. Electrons move around the nucleus. As new tools show, atoms often form well-ordered patterns, or arrays.

What is a scanning tunneling microscope?

_____

_____

Main Idea and Details Where in the atom are the protons, neutrons, and electrons?

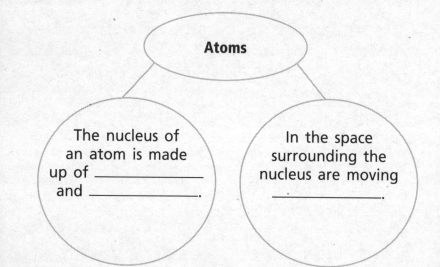

Atoms

The nucleus of an atom is made up of _____ and _____ .

In the space surrounding the nucleus are moving _____ .

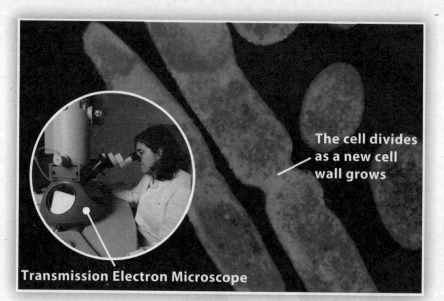

Transmission Electron Microscope

The cell divides as a new cell wall grows

This microscope beams electrons at a thin section of a sample. The large image on this page, with color added, shows the inside parts of _E. coli_.

"Seeing" Atoms

Some microscopes, such as those in your school, use lenses and light to make images larger. Other microscopes form images by using electrons. But neither of these is strong enough to study atoms.

A scanning tunneling microscope (STM) is a kind of electron microscope that is able to "see" atoms. One made the image of silicon atoms shown above. These microscopes have shown scientists how atoms often group together in patterns, or arrays.

MAIN IDEA AND DETAILS

Where in the atom are the protons, neutrons, and electrons?

What Is the Periodic Table?

Scientists have found more than 100 elements. These elements are organized in the periodic table.

Organizing the Elements

Thousands of years ago, people thought there were only four elements: earth, air, fire, and water. But, over time, that changed.

By the 1800s scientists had found many new elements. They were also able to group elements by like properties. But they did not have a way to list the elements.

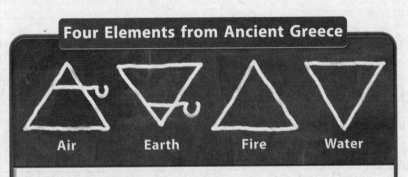

Four Elements from Ancient Greece

Air   Earth   Fire   Water

Scientists long ago used these symbols for what they believed were the four elements—air, earth, fire, and water.

VOCABULARY

chemical symbol an abbreviation of an element's name *(noun)*

metal a shiny substance that can be bent or stretched, and can conduct electricity *(noun)*

noble gas an element that hardly ever combines with another element to form a compound *(noun)*

nonmetal an element, usually in the form of gas, that cannot conduct electricity, does not stretch or bend very much, and can break easily *(noun)*

periodic table the table that logically arranges all known elements *(noun)*

semimetal an element that is like metals in some ways and like a nonmetal in other ways *(noun)*

VOCABULARY SKILL: Prefixes

The prefix *non-* means "not," and the prefix *semi-* means "having some of the characteristics of." Use this information to write your own definitions of *nonmetal* and *semimetal*.

_____

_____

 1.c. Students know that metals have common properties. Some metals are pure elements. Others are combinations of elements.
1.d. Students know that each element is made of one kind of atom. Elements in the periodic table are organized by their chemical properties.

1. Who came up with a way to classify the elements?

_____

2. What does the word *periodic* mean?

_____

_____

I Wonder . . . How might the repeating pattern of the elements in the periodic table be useful for scientists who are searching for new elements?

_____

_____

_____

_____

Mendeleyev's Table

In 1869, a scientist named Dmitri Mendeleyev came up with a way to classify, or list, the elements. He listed them in order of mass. He also put like elements in columns. Though his table was not complete, he thought that one day the missing elements would be discovered and the table would be filled in.

Mendeleyev was right. The modern **periodic table** is a table where the elements are arranged by properties. It is called a periodic table because the properties of the elements have a repeating pattern. The word *periodic* means "repeating."

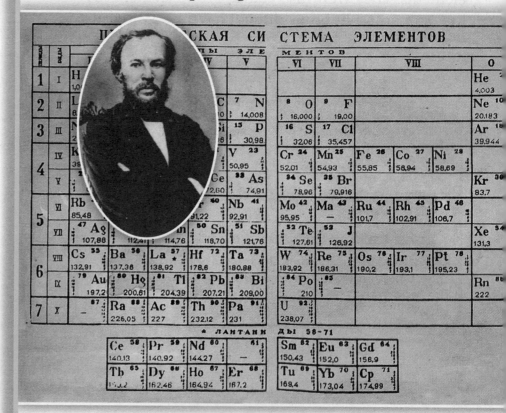

Dmitri Mendeleyev left blank spaces in his table for elements yet to be discovered. This is one of his revised tables.

The Periodic Table

In the periodic table, elements are arranged by their atomic number, which is the number of protons in their nucleus.

An example from the periodic table is shown below. The box for the element carbon shows the atomic number, the chemical symbol, and the name. The **chemical symbol** is an abbreviation, or short form, of the element's name.

Each column within the periodic table is called a group. Elements in a group have properties that are alike. Look at the periodic table on the next page. Find the group that has copper (Cu), silver (Ag), and gold (Au). All these elements are soft, shiny metals.

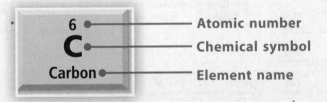

6 — Atomic number
C — Chemical symbol
Carbon — Element name

3. How are elements arranged in the periodic table?

   _____

   _____

4. What is a chemical symbol?

   _____

5. Give two examples of the chemical symbols.

   _____

6. Label the atomic number, chemical symbol, and element name.

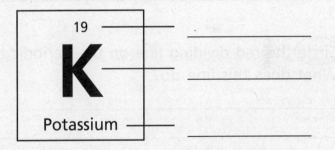

19
K
Potassium

_____

_____

_____

193

7. Look at the key that shows the type of element and the color that represents it. Then draw a line from each color listed below to the type of element it represents.

Yellow   Metals

Blue   Nonmetals

Green   Semimetals

8. List three properties of metals.

a. _____

b. _____

c. _____

9. (Circle) the red dividing line on the periodic table. What does this line do?

_____

_____

194

Metals

Metals are shiny, can be bent or stretched, and can carry electricity. Most elements are metals. Most metal objects are mixtures of different metals. Steel and brass are examples. You can find metals on the periodic table to the left of the red line.

Potassium Potassium is a metal. Bananas have potassium. The cells in your body need potassium.

In the periodic table, colors indicate whether the elements are metals, nonmetals, or semimetals.

Key

6 — Atomic number
C — Chemical symbol
Carbon — Element name

Metallic Properties

Metal
Semimetal
Nonmetal

State at 20°C

C Solid
Br Liquid
Ne Gas

1 H Hydrogen								
3 Li Lithium	4 Be Beryllium							
11 Na Sodium	12 Mg Magnesium							
19 K Potassium	20 Ca Calcium	21 Sc Scandium	22 Ti Titanium	23 V Vanadium	24 Cr Chromium	25 Mn Manganese	26 Fe Iron	27 Co Cobalt
37 Rb Rubidium	38 Sr Strontium	39 Y Yttrium	40 Zr Zirconium	41 Nb Niobium	42 Mo Molybdenum	43 Tc Technetium	44 Ru Ruthenium	45 Rh Rhodium
55 Cs Cesium	56 Ba Barium	57 La Lanthanum	72 Hf Hafnium	73 Ta Tantalum	74 W Tungsten	75 Re Rhenium	76 Os Osmium	77 Ir Iridium
87 Fr Francium	88 Ra Radium	89 Ac Actinium	104 Rf Rutherfordium	105 Db Dubnium	106 Sg Seaborgium	107 Bh Bohrium	108 Hs Hassium	109 Mt Meitnerium

58 Ce Cerium	59 Pr Praseodymium	60 Nd Neodymium	61 Pm Promethium	62 Sm Samarium
90 Th Thorium	91 Pa Protactinium	92 U Uranium	93 Np Neptunium	94 Pu Plutonium

Semimetals

Semimetals are elements that have properties of both metals and nonmetals. They are also known as metalloids.

Silicon Silicon is a semimetal, or metalloid. It is the second-most common element. Sand, rocks, and human bodies all have silicon. Computer chips are made of silicon. Like all semimetals, silicon is a semiconductor. That means it conducts, or carries, electricity some of the time.

						2 He Helium
5 B Boron	6 C Carbon	7 N Nitrogen	8 O Oxygen	9 F Fluorine		10 Ne Neon
13 Al Aluminum	14 Si Silicon	15 P Phosphorus	16 S Sulfur	17 Cl Chlorine		18 Ar Argon

28 Ni Nickel	29 Cu Copper	30 Zn Zinc	31 Ga Gallium	32 Ge Germanium	33 As Arsenic	34 Se Selenium	35 Br Bromine	36 Kr Krypton
46 Pd Palladium	47 Ag Silver	48 Cd Cadmium	49 In Indium	50 Sn Tin	51 Sb Antimony	52 Te Tellurium	53 I Iodine	54 Xe Xenon
78 Pt Platinum	79 Au Gold	80 Hg Mercury	81 Tl Thallium	82 Pb Lead	83 Bi Bismuth	84 Po Polonium	85 At Astatine	86 Rn Radon

63 Eu Europium	64 Gd Gadolinium	65 Tb Terbium	66 Dy Dysprosium	67 Ho Holmium	68 Er Erbium	69 Tm Thulium	70 Yb Ytterbium	71 Lu Lutetium
95 Am Americium	96 Cm Curium	97 Bk Berkelium	98 Cf Californium	99 Es Einsteinium	100 Fm Fermium	101 Md Mendelevium	102 No Nobelium	103 Lr Lawrencium

10. Semimetals have properties of both
_____ and _____.

11. Find and draw a box around silicon on the periodic table.

a. In what natural material would you find silicon?

_____

b. What is an important use of silicon?

_____

12. What is a semiconductor?

_____

_____

Summary Scientists have identified more than 100 elements. They are classified as metals, semimetals, and nonmetals. The elements are organized in the periodic table.

List two ways that nonmetals are different from metals.

a. _____

b. _____

Compare How does the classification of the elements used today compare to that used thousands of years ago?

_____

_____

_____

Signs like this are made of tubes filled with neon and other noble gases. Electricity makes them glow.

Nonmetals and Noble Gases

Nonmetals are elements that cannot conduct electricity, do not stretch or bend, and are easily broken. Nonmetals are mostly solids or gases. The solids are dull looking.

All gases are nonmetals. One gas is oxygen. All humans need oxygen to breathe. There is more oxygen on Earth than any other element.

The column all the way to the right of the periodic table has the noble gases. The **noble gases** are elements that hardly ever combine with other elements to make compounds. Helium is a noble gas. It makes balloons and airships float.

COMPARE

How does today's classification of the elements compare to that used thousands of years ago?

Where Are Elements Found?

Most things on Earth are made of only a few elements.

Rare and Common Elements

Most of the elements on the periodic table are rare. Nearly 99 percent of Earth's crust is made of only eight elements. And almost all of Earth's atmosphere is made of only two: oxygen and nitrogen.

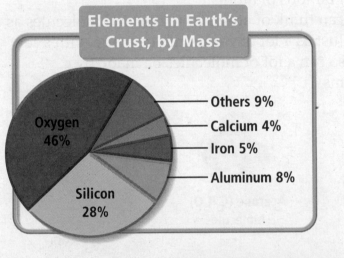

Elements in Earth's Crust, by Mass

- Oxygen 46%
- Silicon 28%
- Others 9%
- Calcium 4%
- Iron 5%
- Aluminum 8%

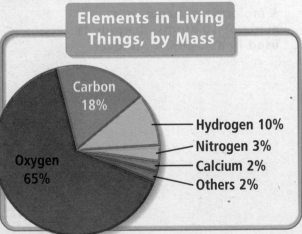

Elements in Living Things, by Mass

- Oxygen 65%
- Carbon 18%
- Hydrogen 10%
- Nitrogen 3%
- Calcium 2%
- Others 2%

VOCABULARY

molecule a group of two or more atoms that are chemically joined and that act as a single unit *(noun)*

VOCABULARY SKILL: Word Origins

The term *molecule* is a noun. The word part *mole* comes from a Latin word meaning "mass." The word part *-cule* is a Latin suffix meaning "tiny" or "small." Use this information to write a definition for *molecule*.

_____

_____

_____

 1.b. Students know that matter is made of atoms. Atoms may combine to form molecules.
1.h. Students know that living things and most materials are made of just a few elements.

1. Complete the diagram to tell about molecules.

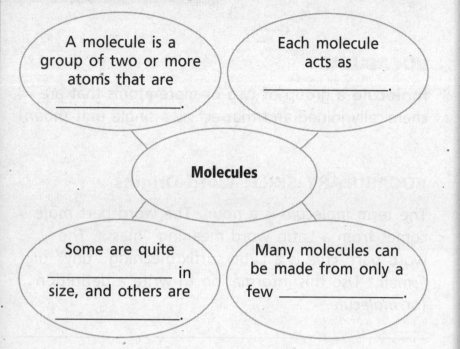

A molecule is a group of two or more atoms that are _____.

Each molecule acts as _____.

Molecules

Some are quite _____ in size, and others are _____.

Many molecules can be made from only a few _____.

2. What kind and how many atoms join to form water?

_____

_____

Molecules

As you have read, elements can combine, or join, to form a large number of compounds. All compounds are made of molecules. A **molecule** is a group of two or more atoms that are chemically joined. They act as a single unit.

Some molecules are small. You learned that water is made of two elements. A water molecule is made of two hydrogen atoms and one oxygen atom.

Other molecules are big. Some in your body are made of billions of atoms!

You can think of atoms as letters and molecules as words. Just as a lot of words can be made with a few letters, so can a lot of molecules be made by a few atoms.

Acetone (C_3H_6O) molecule

A molecule of acetone is made of 10 atoms. Acetone is used in nail-polish remover.

Carbon Compounds

Carbon forms nearly 10 million compounds. Besides mixing with hydrogen to form fuel and plastic, carbon compounds are also the main parts of all living things. They fall into four groups.

- Carbohydrates give the body energy.
- Proteins help build muscle and other tissues.
- Lipids make up fat tissue.
- Nucleic acids help living things grow and develop.

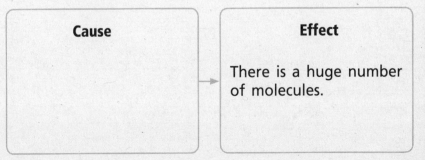

Carbon compounds are everywhere. They help make the sugar in fruit, the muscle in frogs, and the fuel in cars.

CAUSE AND EFFECT

There are only a few elements. Why are there a huge number of molecules?

Summary Most things on Earth are made of only a few elements—far fewer than the more than 100 elements that scientists have discovered. Molecules are made of two or more atoms chemically joined.

Complete the chart to tell about carbon compounds, which are the main parts of all living things.

Carbon Compounds	What It Does
Carbohydrates	
	help build muscle and other tissues
Lipids	
	help living things grow and develop

 Cause and Effect There are only a few elements. Why are there a huge number of molecules?

Cause	Effect
	There is a huge number of molecules.

199

Use the periodic table on page 194 to draw a carbon atom. Make sure the number of protons equals the number of electrons.

Glossary

atom the smallest particle of an element that still has the properties of that element

átomo en un elemento, la partícula más pequeña que tiene las propiedades de ese elemento

chemical symbol an abbreviation of an element's name

símbolo químico abreviatura del nombre de un elemento

compound a pure substance made of two or more elements that are chemically combined

compuesto sustancia pura formada por dos o más elementos combinados químicamente

electron a negatively charged particle that moves in the space around the nucleus of an atom

electrón partícula con carga negativa que se mueve en el espacio que rodea el núcleo de un átomo

element a substance that cannot be broken apart chemically into other substances

elemento sustancia que no puede dividirse químicamente en otras sustancias

metal a shiny substance that can be bent or stretched, and can conduct electricity

metal sustancia brillante que se puede doblar o estirar y que conduce electricidad

molecule a group of two or more atoms that are chemically joined and that act as a single unit

molécula grupo de dos o más átomos unidos químicamente y que actúan como una sola unidad

Glossary

neutron an atomic particle that lacks charge

    neutrón partícula atómica sin carga

noble gas an element that hardly ever combines with another element to form a compound

    gas noble elemento que es difícil combinar con otro elemento para formar un compuesto

nonmetal an element, usually in the form of gas, that cannot conduct electricity, does not stretch or bend very much, and can break easily

    no metal un elemento, generalmente en forma de gas, que no conduce la electricidad, no se dobla o estira mucho y que se rompe con facilidad

nucleus (NOO klee uhs) the structure in the center of an atom that contains protons and neutrons

    núcleo estructura en el centro de un átomo que contiene protones y neutrones

periodic table the table that logically arranges all known elements

    tabla periódica tabla que ordena de forma lógica todos los elementos conocidos

proton a small, positively-charged atomic particle

    protón pequeña partícula atómica de carga positiva

semimetal an element that is like a metal in some ways and like nonmetal in other ways

    semimetal un elemento que tiene características de los metales y de los no metales

 Visit www.eduplace.com to play puzzles and word games.

Circle the words in this Glossary that are the same in Spanish and English.

KWL

WHAT DID YOU LEARN?

Vocabulary

❶ (Circle) the correct answer on the page.

Comprehension

❷ _____

❸ _____

❹ _____

_____

Critical Thinking

❺ _____

_____

_____

Responding

Think About What You Have Read

Vocabulary

❶ The center of an atom is called the _____.

   A) nucleus

   B) proton

   C) element

   D) neutron

Comprehension

❷ Elements called _____ are usually shiny, can be bent or stretched, and conduct electricity.

❸ In the periodic table, elements are arranged according to _____.

❹ What is a scanning tunneling microscope?

Critical Thinking

❺ What information about an element can you figure out from its location on the periodic table?

WHAT DO YOU KNOW?

List one fact that you know about each of these topics.

a. Compounds _____

_____

b. Acids _____

_____

c. Bases _____

_____

d. Salts _____

_____

Chemical Compounds

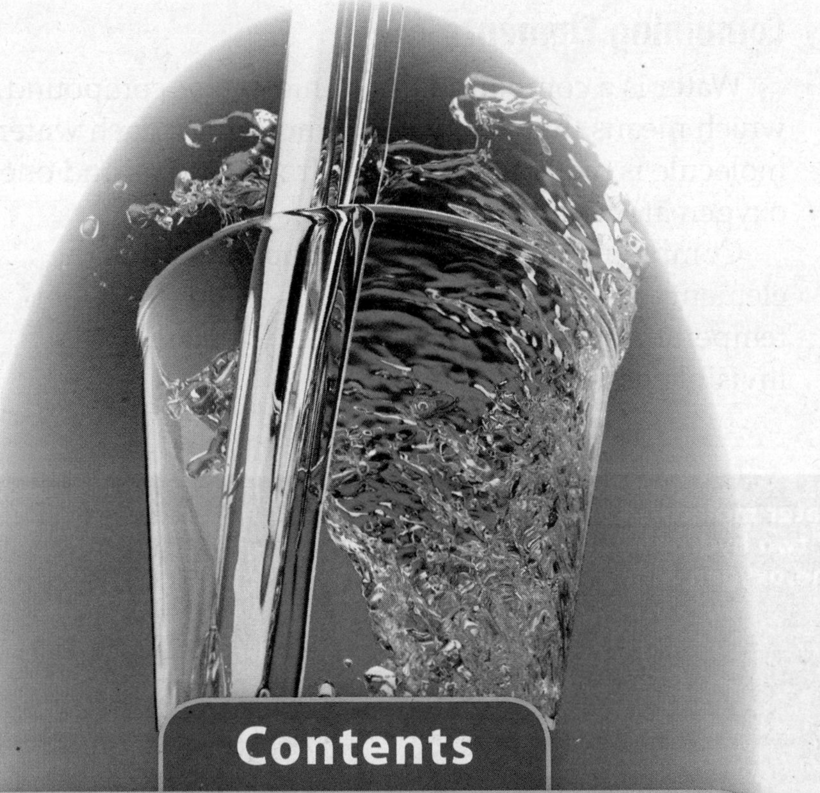

Contents

KWL

WHAT DO YOU WANT TO KNOW?

Look at the pictures and headings in this chapter. Then list one thing you want to find out about each of the following topics.

a. Compounds _____

_____

b. Acids _____

_____

c. Bases _____

_____

d. Salts _____

_____

VOCABULARY

chemical formula a shorthand way to describe a compound *(noun)*

chemical reaction a process in which one or more substances are changed into one or more different substances *(noun)*

VOCABULARY SKILL: Prefixes

Many English words have prefixes. The word *subscript* has the prefix *sub-*, which means "below" or "under." The base word of *subscript* is *script,* which means "something written." Together, they mean "something written below." Parts of chemical formulas, such as H_2O, are written as subscripts. What is the subscript in the formula H_2O? Why is this a subscript?

_____

_____

1.a. Students know that chemical reactions result in products with different properties.
1.b. Students know that matter is made of atoms. Atoms may combine to form molecules.
1.f. Students know that differences in chemical and physical properties are used to separate mixtures and identify compounds.

---

1 | What Are Compounds?

Two or more elements can combine to make a compound. Compounds have different properties than the elements that make them up.

Combining Elements

Water is a compound. It is a molecular compound, which means that it is made of molecules. Each water molecule is made up of two hydrogen atoms and one oxygen atom.

Compounds have different properties from the elements that make them. Water is a liquid at room temperature. But hydrogen and oxygen are both invisible gases.

Water molecules are made up of two hydrogen atoms and one oxygen atom.

Many Compounds

Some compounds, such as water, are made of just two elements. Others, such as limestone rock, are made of more. Look at the odd forms of limestone in this picture of a cave. Limestone is mostly a compound called calcium carbonate. The same compound makes the hard shells of some animals.

Another familiar compound is iron oxide. You may know it as rust. When steel is exposed to water and air, the iron in it will rust. Salt speeds up rusting.

The limestone rock that forms this cave is made of the compound calcium carbonate.

Some of the iron in this truck has rusted. Rust is a compound called iron oxide.

1. Look at the picture of the cave.

   a. What type of rock is found in the cave?

   _____

   b. What compound makes up this rock?

   _____

2. Look at the picture of the truck.

   a. What is the brown substance on the surface of the truck?

   _____

   b. What compound makes up this substance?

   _____

3. In a chemical reaction, one substance is changed into one or more _____ _____.

4. Fill in the diagram below to learn about the breakdown of sugar into simpler substances.

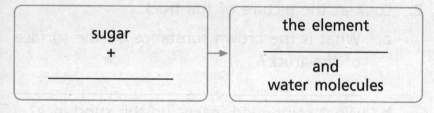

sugar
+
_____

→

the element
_____
and
water molecules

Making and Breaking Compounds

In order for a compound to form, elements must take part in a chemical reaction. A **chemical reaction** is a process in which one or more substances are changed into one or more different substances. This is also known as a chemical change.

Some chemical reactions break down compounds into simpler substances. Look at the pictures below. If you heat sugar long enough, a chemical reaction will occur. It will release water vapor to the air and leave behind carbon. In other reactions, simple substances combine to form more complex ones.

Chemical Reaction

1 Sucrose ($C_{12}H_{22}O_{11}$) is a sugar, a compound of carbon, hydrogen, and oxygen.

2 When heated, the sucrose molecules break down, leaving the element carbon and releasing water molecules.

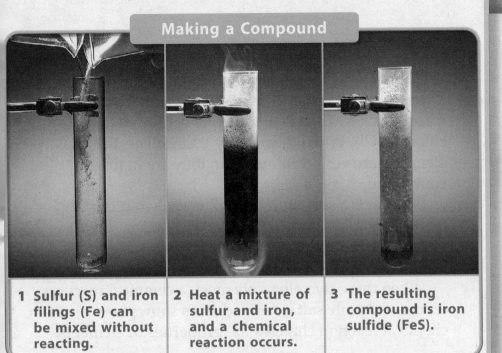

Making a Compound

1 Sulfur (S) and iron filings (Fe) can be mixed without reacting.

2 Heat a mixture of sulfur and iron, and a chemical reaction occurs.

3 The resulting compound is iron sulfide (FeS).

Compounds and Formulas

Sometimes elements need something to make them react. In the pictures above, you see that when iron and sulfur are mixed, nothing happens. They remain separate elements. However, when you heat the mixture, the elements become the compound iron sulfide.

Chemical formulas are used to identify chemical compounds. A **chemical formula** is a short and easy way to write a compound using chemical symbols and numbers.

Fe is the symbol for iron, and S is the symbol for sulfur. So, the chemical formula when they react is FeS. Water is written H_2O. This formula shows that there are two atoms of hydrogen in water to only one of oxygen. The way the 2 is written is called a subscript.

5. Fill in the diagram below to learn about how compounds are made.

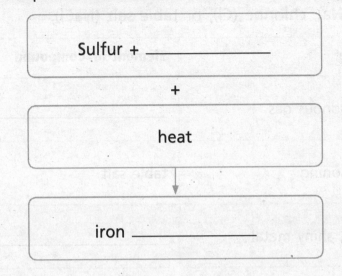

Sulfur + _____

+

heat

iron _____

6. Circle the chemical formula of the compound formed.

Fe   S   O   H   FeS

7. Use the clues in the chart to determine the element or compound. Choose from sodium (Na), chlorine (Cl), or table salt (NaCl).

Clue	Element or Compound
poisonous gas	_____
seasoning	table salt
soft, shiny metal	_____

8. Look at the photo. (Circle) the harmless compound. How does table salt being formed show that a chemical reaction changes the properties of elements?

_____

_____

_____

_____

Everyday Compounds

You see and use some compounds all the time. Salt is one of them. Salt is known scientifically as sodium chloride, or NaCl. It is made up of sodium (Na) and chlorine (Cl). When they are by themselves, the two elements are very different than they are in the compound.

Sodium is a soft, shiny metal. It easily reacts with many substances. When it mixes with water, it reacts violently. Chlorine on its own is a poisonous gas. It is used to kill bacteria in drinking water.

When these two elements meet, a chemical reaction occurs and table salt is formed. This shows how a chemical reaction changes the properties of elements.

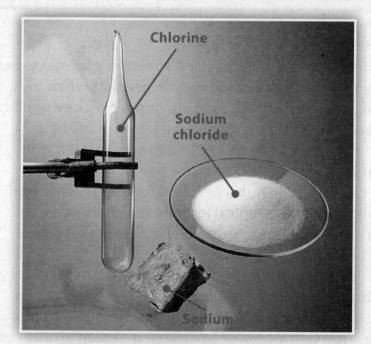

SODIUM CHLORIDE
Sodium (Na) and chlorine (Cl) are the elements that make up the compound sodium chloride (NaCl), or table salt.

The snow and ice stay frozen because the temperature is below 0°C (32°F), the freezing point of water.

Water: Earth's Most Abundant Compound

Almost three quarters of Earth is covered with water. All organisms need water to live.

Water is everywhere. But it is also very special. It is one of the few compounds that is a liquid at room temperature. It also dissolves a great many other substances, which means that the other substances mix evenly with the water.

MAIN IDEA AND DETAILS

What forms when atoms of two or more elements combine chemically?

Summary The properties of a compound differ from those of the elements that make it up. Water is a unique compound that is found everywhere on Earth. List two properties that make water unique.

a. _____

_____

b. _____

_____

Main Ideas and Details What forms when atoms of two or more elements combine chemically?

_____

_____

VOCABULARY

boiling point the temperature at which enough energy is added to a liquid to change it into a gas *(noun)*

chemical property the ability or tendency of material to change its chemical makeup *(noun)*

conductivity a material's ability to carry heat or electricity *(noun)*

density that mass per unit volume of a material *(noun)*

melting point the temperature at which a solid substance changes to a liquid *(noun)*

physical property any characteristic of matter that can be measured or detected by the senses *(noun)*

solubility the measure of how much of one substance can dissolve in another *(noun)*

2 What Are Some Properties of Compounds?

Physical and chemical properties are used to describe and identify matter.

Using Your Senses

You can use your senses to describe the properties of matter. You might describe a piece of ice as cold, with no smell or color. Smoke from a campfire might look gray and have no shape, but it would also smell familiar, or well known.

WATER BOTTLE
The plastic is dark, lightweight, and flexible. Unlike glass, it won't break when you drop it.

SHOES
Tough, sturdy spikes dig into the ground. The shoe is softer inside, where the foot fits.

1.f. Students know that differences in chemical and physical properties are used to separate mixtures and identify compounds.

There are two ways the properties of matter can be described: physical properties and chemical properties.

A **physical property** can be measured or noticed by the senses. Some physical properties are size, color, and smell. Many physical properties, such as mass and volume, can be measured.

A **chemical property** is the ability of something to change its chemical makeup. You can find the chemical properties of something by watching how it changes under certain conditions. If a piece of paper is held in a fire, the paper will burn. Burning is a chemical change. It makes new matter that is very different from the paper.

Some Properties of Materials		
Property	**Water**	**Glass**
Color	colorless and clear	colorless and clear
State	liquid at room temperature	solid at room temperature
Melting point	0°C	may be greater than 1,000°C
Conductivity	conducts electricity	does not conduct electricity
Reactivity with sodium hydroxide	dissolves sodium hydroxide	reacts with sodium hydroxide, which etches the glass

1. Fill in the Venn diagram to compare and contrast physical properties and chemical properties.

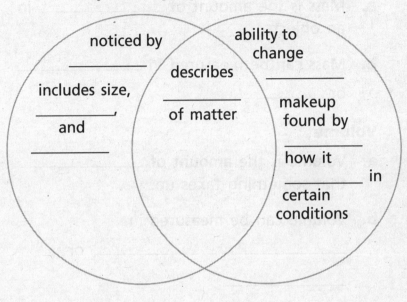

Physical Property   **Chemical Property**

noticed by _____

includes size, _____, and _____

describes _____ of matter

ability to change _____

makeup found by _____ how it _____ in certain conditions

2. Look at the table. Circle the physical properties of water. Draw a box around the chemical properties of glass.

3. Complete the outline to describe physical properties.

Mass

a. Mass is the amount of _____ in an object.

b. Mass can be measured in _____ or _____.

Volume

a. Volume is the amount of _____ that something takes up.

b. Volume can be measured in _____ _____ or _____.

Density

The density of a material is its _____ per unit _____.

Mass, Volume, and Density

Mass is the amount of matter in an object. It is measured in grams (g) or kilograms (kg).

Volume is the amount of space that something takes up. It is measured in cubic centimeters (cm^3) or milliliters (mL).

The **density** of a material is its mass per unit volume. Imagine you have two baseball bats that are the same size. The only difference is that one is made out of plastic foam and the other is made out of wood. You know that the wood bat would have more mass. Why? Because even though they take up the same amount of space, wood is denser than foam.

Some Physical Properties

VOLUME	MASS	DENSITY
To find the volume of a solid that does not float in water, measure the volume of water that it displaces, or moves. The volume of the orange is the difference of the two water levels.	The mass of an object can be measured with a balance. Here, the mass of the can equals the sum of the two masses in the right pan.	A bottle filled with plastic foam will float because the foam is less dense than water. A bottle filled with sand will sink because sand is denser than water.

Melting and Boiling Points

Another physical property is state of matter. The three common states are solid, liquid, and gas.

Solids have a definite shape and volume. Liquids flow. They take on the shape of what holds them, like water in a glass. But liquids do keep the same volume. Gases have no set shape or volume. They can shrink or grow to fill anything. Gases are less dense than liquids or solids.

The temperature at which a solid changes to a liquid is its **melting point**. When enough energy is added to a liquid, it will turn into a gas. The temperature at which a liquid changes to a gas is its **boiling point**. The melting point and boiling point of a substance never change.

BOILING POINT
The boiling point of water is 100°C.

MELTING POINT
The melting point of water is 0°C.

4. Write *solid, liquid, gas, melting point,* or *boiling point* next to each of the clues below.

_____ has ability to flow

_____ temperature at which a solid changes to a liquid

_____ has no set shape or volume

_____ has a definite shape and volume

_____ temperature at which a liquid changes to gas

5. Circle the boiling point on the thermometer. Draw a box around the melting point of water on the thermometer.

215

Summary Physical and chemical properties are used to describe and identify matter. Solubility is the measure of how much of one substance can dissolve in another. The conductivity of a material is its ability to carry energy. Fill in the Venn diagram below to compare and contrast solubility and conductivity.

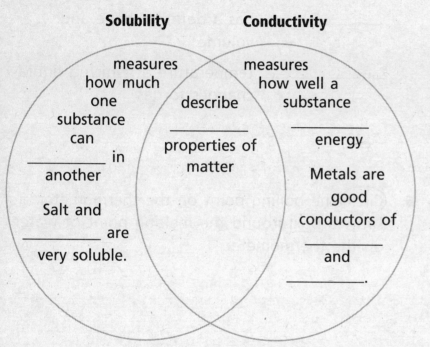

Solubility   **Conductivity**

measures how much one substance can _____ in another

Salt and _____ are very soluble.

describe _____ properties of matter

measures how well a substance _____ energy

Metals are good conductors of _____ and _____.

Main Idea and Details Under what conditions does a substance change state?

_____

_____

216

Solubility and Conductivity

If you stir sugar in water it will dissolve, which means that the sugar will mix evenly with the water. **Solubility** is the measure of how much of one substance can dissolve in another. Solubility is a physical property of matter. Some substances, such as sugar and salt, are very soluble in water. Others, such as oil and sand, are not.

Another physical property of matter is conductivity. **Conductivity** measures how well a substance carries energy. Most metals are good conductors of both electricity and heat. Their conductivity is high. Rubber and plastic do not conduct well at all.

Solubility

Oil and sand will not dissolve in water, so they form separate layers when mixed with water.

Powdered drink mix will dissolve in water, so the two form a colored solution when mixed.

MAIN IDEA AND DETAILS

Under what conditions does a substance change state?

What Are Acids, Bases, and Salts?

3

Acids, bases, and salts are kinds of compounds. You can measure how strong an acid or base is with the pH scale.

Acids and Bases

Both lemon juice and vinegar taste sour. They taste like that because they have acid in them. But acids are not just in food. Your stomach uses acid. So does a car battery.

Bases are used in cleaners, such as soap and bleach. If you were to taste a base, it would taste bitter.

Acids and bases are important kinds of compounds.

Acids

PROPERTIES OF ACIDS
- taste sour
- turn blue litmus paper red
- release hydrogen ions (H⁺)
- react easily with other substances, especially bases

EXAMPLES OF ACIDS
many fruits and fruit juices, battery acid, vinegar, stomach acid, soft drinks, sour milk

VOCABULARY

acid a compound that typically releases hydrogen ions *(noun)*

base a compound that typically accepts hydrogen ions *(noun)*

indicator a substance used to show the presence of an acid or a base in a substance *(noun)*

pH (potential of hydrogen) the value of measured strength of acids and bases *(noun)*

salt a compound formed when a strong acid reacts with a strong base *(noun)*

VOCABULARY SKILL: Word Origins

The word *acid* comes from the Latin word *acidus*, which means "sour." Sometimes people refer to others as being *acid-tongued*. Based on the origin of the word *acid*, write a definition for the word *acid-tongued*.

 1.a. Students know that chemical reactions result in products with different properties.
1.f. Students know that differences in chemical and physical properties are used to separate mixtures and identify compounds.
1.i. Students know the common properties of salts.

217

Write *acid*, *base*, *pH*, or *indicator* next to the clues below.

_____ compound that accepts hydrogen ions

_____ compound that releases hydrogen ions

_____ measures the strength of an acid or base

_____ changes color when it touches an acid or base

I Wonder . . . People use baking soda to make pastries. A mixture of baking soda and water turns red litmus paper blue. It has a pH level of 8. Is baking soda an acid or a base? What do you think?

_____

_____

_____

Ions are atoms that have lost or gained one or more electrons. An **acid** releases hydrogen ions. A **base** accepts hydrogen ions.

You should never taste something to see if it is an acid or a base. Instead use an acid-base indicator. An **indicator** changes color when it touches an acid or a base. Litmus paper is a common indicator.

To measure the strength of an acid or base, scientists use a **pH** scale. The scale centers on the number 7, which is the pH of water. Acids have a pH lower than 7. Bases have a pH higher than 7.

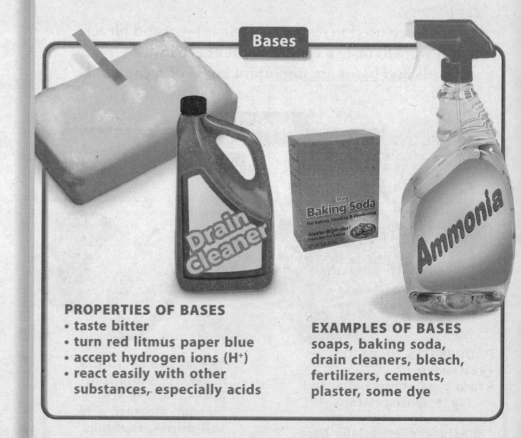

Bases

PROPERTIES OF BASES
- taste bitter
- turn red litmus paper blue
- accept hydrogen ions (H^+)
- react easily with other substances, especially acids

EXAMPLES OF BASES
soaps, baking soda, drain cleaners, bleach, fertilizers, cements, plaster, some dye

Sea salt, shown here, is taken from the ocean.

Salts

When a strong acid reacts with a strong base, they make a salt. **Salts** are compounds made from a metal and a nonmetal. There are more kinds of salt than the one you use when you eat. Many salts are hard and brittle. Most dissolve in water.

COMPARE AND CONTRAST

How do acids and bases differ?

Summary Salts are formed when a strong acid reacts with a strong base. Put an X next to each true statement about salts.

_____ Salt is typically made from a metal and a nonmetal.

_____ Few salts dissolve in water.

_____ Table salt is the only type of salt that exists.

_____ Many salts are hard and brittle.

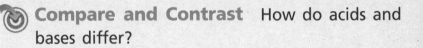 **Compare and Contrast** How do acids and bases differ?

_____

_____

_____

Group two or more of the words on the page and explain why they go together.

acid a compound that typically releases hydrogen ions

 ácido un compuesto que, por lo general, libera iones de hidrógeno

base a compound that typically receives hydrogen ions

 base compuesto que, por lo general, recibe iones de hidrógeno

boiling point the temperature at which enough energy is added to a liquid to change it into a gas

 punto de ebullición temperatura a la que se añade suficiente energía a un líquido para convertirlo en gas

chemical formula a shorthand way to describe a compound

 fórmula química forma abreviada de describir un compuesto

chemical property the ability or tendency of material to change its chemical makeup

 propiedad química capacidad o tendencia de un material para cambiar su composición química

chemical reaction a process in which one or more substances are changed into one or more different substances

 reacción química proceso mediante el cual una o más sustancias se transforman en otra u otras sustancias distintas

conductivity a material's ability to carry heat or electricity

 conductividad capacidad de un material para transportar calor o electricidad

Glossary

density the mass per unit volume of a material

densidad masa por unidad de volumen de un material

indicator a substance used to show the presence of an acid or a base in a substance

indicador sustancia que se usa para identificar la presencia de ácidos o bases

melting point the temperature at which a solid substance changes to a liquid

punto de fusión temperatura a la cual un sólido cambia a líquido

pH (potential of hydrogen) the value of measured strength of acids and bases

pH (potencial de hidrógeno) valor de la fuerza medida en ácidos y bases

physical property any characteristic of matter that can be measured or detected by the senses

propiedad física cualquier característica de la materia que pueda ser medida o detectada a través de los sentidos

salt a compound formed when a strong acid reacts with a strong base

sal compuesto que se forma cuando un ácido fuerte reacciona con una base fuerte

solubility the measure of how much of one substance can dissolve in another

solubilidad medida de la cantidad de sustancia que puede disolverse en otra sustancia

 Visit www.eduplace.com to play puzzles and word games.

Circle the words in this glossary that are the same in English and Spanish.

Chapter Review

KWL

WHAT DID YOU LEARN?

Vocabulary

❶ (Circle) the correct answer on the page.

Comprehension

❷ _____

❸ _____

❹ _____

_____

Critical Thinking

❺ _____

_____

_____

_____

Think About What You Have Read

Vocabulary

❶ The color of a substance is an example of a/an _____.

   A) indicator

   B) chemical property

   C) physical property

   D) pH

Comprehension

❷ The temperature at which a liquid changes to a gas is its _____.

❸ What is one product of a reaction between a strong acid and a strong base?

❹ Choose two objects. Describe and compare their properties.

Critical Thinking

❺ You have two liquids, both clear and colorless. Describe a sample test to determine if they are the same or different. To run the test, you may use a balance, hot plate, barometer, thermometer, and anything else you wish.

WHAT DO YOU KNOW?

Write something you know about each of the states of matter.

a. solid _____

_____

_____

b. liquid _____

_____

_____

c. gas _____

_____

_____

Tell something you know about mixtures and solutions.

_____

_____

_____

Characteristics of Matter

Contents

KWL

WHAT DO YOU WANT TO KNOW?

Skim the pictures and headings in this chapter. Write one question you have about each of these topics.

a. States of matter _____

_____

_____

b. Mixtures _____

_____

_____

c. Chemical changes in matter _____

_____

_____

VOCABULARY

gas a form of matter that has no definite shape or volume *(noun)*

liquid a form of matter that has a definite volume, but no definite shape *(noun)*

solid a form of matter that has a definite shape and volume *(noun)*

VOCABULARY SKILL: Word Origins

The word *liquid* comes from the Latin *liquidus*, which means "to be fluid" or "to flow freely." Rewrite the definition of *liquid*, using the word *fluid*.

_____

_____

1.b. Students know that matter is made of atoms. Atoms may combine to form molecules.
1.g. Students know that solids, liquids, and gases have distinct properties.

1 What Are Three States of Matter?

Matter can exist in three states: solid, liquid, and gas. These states depend on how particles in matter move and how they are arranged.

Solids, Liquids, and Gases

A state of matter is the physical form that matter takes. The three states of matter are solid, liquid, and gas.

Look at the picture below. In it, ice is matter in the solid state. Ocean water is in the liquid state. You cannot see it, but the air above the water is a mix of gases. Water vapor is one of these gases. Water vapor is water in the gas state.

Water can exist as a solid, liquid, or gas. In each state, the particles of matter are arranged in predictable ways.

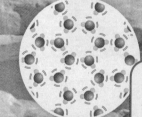

SOLIDS
In solids, particles are held together very closely. They vibrate in place.

Particles and State of Matter

You know that matter is made of atoms and molecules. These particles are always moving.

The state of all matter depends on how the particles move and how far apart they are. In solids, the particles are packed tightly together and they vibrate, or shake, back and forth.

In liquids, the particles are still very close together. But, unlike solids, they do have a little space they can move in.

In gases, the particles are very far apart. These gas particles are free to move, and they bounce off one another all the time.

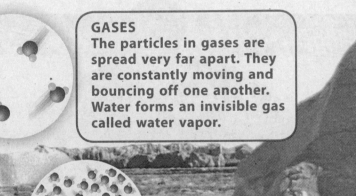

GASES
The particles in gases are spread very far apart. They are constantly moving and bouncing off one another. Water forms an invisible gas called water vapor.

LIQUIDS
In the liquid state, water particles can slip past one another and move about.

1. List the three states of matter.

   a. _____

   b. _____

   c. _____

2. Identify the state of matter by the description of its particles.

   a. _____ Particles are packed together tightly and vibrate in place.

   b. _____ Particles are close together, but with a little space; they can slip past one another and move about.

   c. _____ Particles are spread far apart and are constantly moving and bouncing off one another.

227

3. List two properties of solids.

a. _____

b. _____

4. Why do some solids, such as a foam pillow, seem to change shape?

_____

_____

_____

_____

Solids

A **solid** is a kind of matter that has a set shape and volume. The way the particles are tightly packed and the way that they vibrate give solids their properties.

Solids keep their shape. No matter where you set a block of wood, it will still be a block of wood. Another property of solids is their definite volume. That means they take up the same amount of space no matter where they are.

Some solids, such as foam or a pillow, seem as if they change their shape. They really do not. These solids move because of air pockets within them.

You can use a foam football because of the air inside it. The solid parts inside the foam keep the same size and shape. So do other solids, such as wood, ice, cloth, and metal.

This liquid was poured into different containers. It changed shape but kept its volume of 50 mL.

Liquids

A **liquid** is a form of matter that has a set volume, but no set shape. A liquid has no shape because its particles are not held together. They can flow past one another. This means a liquid is fluid. So, a liquid changes shape to match its container.

Liquids have a set volume. Look at the picture above. While the liquid changes its shape every time, the volume stays the same.

5. Compare and contrast solids and liquids.

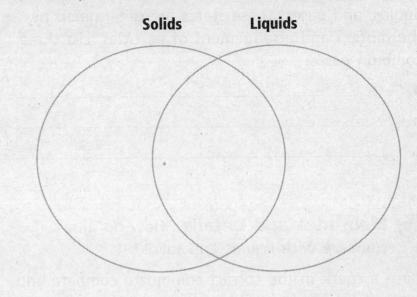

Solids   Liquids

I Wonder . . . Judging from its physical properties, is oil a solid or liquid? What do you think?

_____

_____

_____

_____

Summary Matter can exist in three states: solids, liquids, and gases. These states are determined by the motion and arrangement of particles. List three common gases.

a. _____

b. _____

c. _____

Main Idea and Details How do gases compare with liquids and solids?

Place a check in the correct column to compare and contrast liquids and solids.

Matter	Definite Shape	No Definite Shape	Definite Volume	No Definite Volume
Solid				
Liquid				

Gases

A **gas** is a form of matter with no definite shape or volume. Common gases include oxygen, nitrogen, and carbon dioxide.

The particles that make up a gas move around freely and bounce into each other. When put into a container, a gas will spread out to fill the container and take its shape. The gas will flow, which means it is fluid.

States of Matter			
Property	Solid	Liquid	Gas
Definite shape	yes	no	no
Definite volume	yes	yes	no
Fluid	no	yes	yes
Particle spacing	close	close	varies

The spacing and speed of particles determine state of matter.

MAIN IDEA AND DETAILS

How do gases compare with liquids and solids?

What Are Mixtures and Solutions?

In a mixture, the parts keep their physical properties. Mixtures whose particles are evenly combined are called solutions.

Types of Mixtures

A **mixture** is a combination of two or more substances, but it is different from a compound. The substances in a mixture are not chemically combined as they are in a compound. There is no chemical reaction.

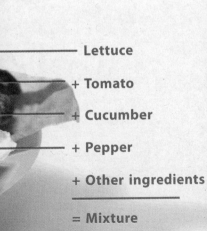

A salad is a mixture. The different parts that make up the mixture have different properties.

— Lettuce

+ Tomato

+ Cucumber

+ Pepper

+ Other ingredients

= Mixture

VOCABULARY

mixture a physical combination of two or more substances *(noun)*

solution a mixture in which parts are evenly distributed at the level of atoms or molecules *(noun)*

VOCABULARY SKILL: Word Origins

An *alloy* is a type of mixture you will learn about in this lesson. *Alloy* comes from the Latin *alligare*, which means "to bind one thing to another" and from an Old French term *aleier*, which means "to mix with a baser metal." From this information, what do you think an alloy is?

_____

_____

 1.c. Students know that metals have common properties. Some metals are pure elements. Others are combinations of elements.
1.f. Students know that differences in chemical and physical properties are used to separate mixtures and identify compounds.

231

1. In a mixture, the parts keep their _____ properties.

2. Why can you separate a mixture of corks and marbles by placing them in water?

_____

_____

_____

Separating a Mixture

In a mixture, each substance keeps its properties. So, mixtures can be separated by different properties.

Imagine a mixture of corks and marbles. It would take time to pick out all the cork pieces. But, because cork floats in water, you can separate the mixture quickly by putting it in water. All the marbles will sink and the corks will float. You have separated the mixture by its properties.

Corks and marbles

To separate a mixture, take advantage of the physical properties of the different parts.

Mixture or Compound?

The parts of a mixture can be present in differing amounts. Say that you like salad with a lot of lettuce and onions, and your friend likes it with very little lettuce and extra tomatoes. Even though you like differing amounts of the contents, you both have a salad. They are both mixtures.

A compound always has the same amount of each item. Every molecule of water has one oxygen atom and two hydrogen atoms. These things cannot change. If they do, it is not water anymore.

This bowl of fruits and nuts is a mixture because each substance keeps its properties. The nuts are still nuts, even though they are mixed with fruit.

3. Look at the list. Classify each item as a mixture or compound.

_____ air

_____ water

_____ salt and sugar

_____ salt

_____ sugar

_____ nuts and bolts

4. Circle the word that will make each sentence true.

a. A solution is a (compound, mixture).

b. In a solution, the parts that make it up are (evenly, unevenly) distributed.

5. a. What is a solute?

_____

b. What is a solvent?

_____

6. Look at the photos of the iodine-alcohol solution being made. Circle the label of the substance that is the solute. Draw a box around the label of the substance that is the solvent.

Iodine

Alcohol

When iodine crystals are added to alcohol, the crystals begin to dissolve. In a short time, the solution is a uniform purple.

Solutions

A **solution** is a mixture in which the particles of the substances that make up the mixture are evenly spread out. The particles that are evenly spread out, or distributed, are at the level of atoms or molecules.

You can make a solution with powdered lemonade mix and water. Sugar and flavoring particles mix with the water to make the lemonade solution. And if it is mixed well, all the sips will taste the same. All the particles will be evenly distributed in the solution.

In any solution, the substance being dissolved, such as the powdered lemonade, is the solute. The substance that dissolves the solute, such as the water, is called a solvent.

Separating a Solution

In order to separate a solution, it helps to know the properties of the materials that were mixed. You know that water evaporates. So, if you are trying to separate salt from sea water, you can leave the water in the air for a couple days. The water will evaporate. You will find only crystals of salt.

Another way to separate materials is by knowing their different melting and boiling points. This is how sugar is collected. Sugar cane juice is taken from the sugar cane plant. The juice is made of water and sugar. Knowing that the boiling point of water is lower than that of sugar, you can boil the juice. This removes the water and leaves the sugar behind.

Sugar from Sugar Cane

First, the cane is prepared for juicing.

Sugar cane juice contains a solution of sugar and water.

Water is removed from the juice, and solid sugar is recovered.

---

7. What should you know in order to separate the materials in a solution?

_____

_____

8. Fill in the missing step in the process of separating salt from sea water.

> Leave the open container of sea water in the air for a couple of days.

↓

>

↓

> Salt crystals are left behind in the container.

Summary In a mixture, the parts keep their physical properties. These properties can be used to separate the mixture. Mixtures made up of parts that are evenly mixed at the atomic or molecular level are called solutions.

What is a mixture of two or more metals called?

Compare and Contrast Compare mixtures and compounds.

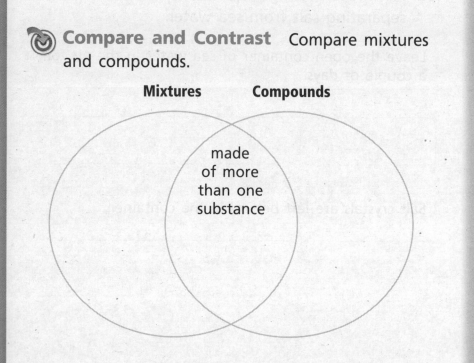

Mixtures   Compounds

made
of more
than one
substance

Alloys

An alloy is a mixture of two or more metals. It can also be the mixture of a metal and another solid. Alloys usually have properties of all the materials that make them.

Bronze is an alloy of the metals copper and tin. It combines the best properties of both. It is easily made into different shapes. For that reason it has been used for hundreds of years in tools and sculptures.

BRASS Many musical instruments are made of alloys such as brass. Brass is made of copper and zinc.

COMPARE AND CONTRAST

Compare mixtures and compounds.

236

How Does Matter Change? **3**

A chemical change in matter changes the identity of the matter. A physical change does not.

Changes in Size and Shape

A physical change is a change in the size, shape, or state of matter. No new matter is formed.

If you sharpen your pencil, you make a physical change. The pencil is a different size than when you started. The shavings, or what is left after you are done, look nothing like the pencil they came from. But the chemical makeup of both the pencil and the shavings are the same.

Cutting

Sanding

Drilling

The students are changing the shape of wood in different ways. Each change is a physical change.

VOCABULARY

condensation the change of state from a gas to a liquid (*noun*)

evaporation the change in state from a liquid to a gas; slow or gradual vaporization (*noun*)

sublimation the process of a solid changing directly to a gas without passing through the liquid state (*noun*)

vaporization the process of a liquid changing into a gas (*noun*)

VOCABULARY SKILL: Antonyms

Antonyms are words with opposite meanings. Find a pair of antonyms in the vocabulary list. Write them below.

_____

 1.f. Students know that differences in chemical and physical properties are used to separate mixtures and identify compounds.
1.g. Students know that solids, liquids, and gases have distinct properties.

1. Define *physical change*.

_____

_____

2. Complete the chart to show how temperature changes most matter.

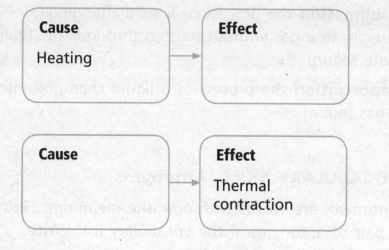

Cause		Effect
Heating	→	

Cause		Effect
	→	Thermal contraction

3. How does water change when it freezes?

_____

The liquid in this can froze.

Expansion and Contraction

Most matter expands, or increases in size, when it is heated. This is called thermal expansion. Most matter contracts, or decreases in size, when it is cooled. This is called thermal contraction.

Water does not contract when it is cooled. Water expands when it freezes and its volume increases. That is why ice floats on top of water.

Have you ever seen a soda or juice can after it has been left out in the cold too long? The can will split or even explode! The molecules of water in ice take up more space than they do in liquid water. When the water freezes, it expands. This increase in the volume of the water makes it too big to fit in the can.

Heating and cooling change the volume of matter, but they do not change the mass, or weight.

Melting and Freezing

In many places, spring brings warmer temperatures. Snow and ice begin to change from a solid to a liquid. This change of state, called melting, is a physical change. The substance, water, stays the same chemically.

When winter comes again, temperatures get colder. Water changes from a liquid to a solid. This physical change is called freezing.

When spring arrives, winter snow melts and forms liquid water.

Liquid water

Snow

4. Complete the sequence chart about melting and freezing.

Winter ends. Spring brings _____ temperatures.

Ice begins to change from a _____ to a _____. This change is called _____.

When winter comes again, temperatures are again cold. Liquid water changes to a _____. This change is called _____.

5. Vaporization is the change of state from a

_____ to a _____.

6. Slow or gradual vaporization is called

_____.

7. Very fast vaporization is called _____.

Vaporizing and Condensing

Watch a drop of water on a hot frying pan. It will sizzle, pop, and disappear. The change of state is caused by a quick temperature change.

By adding energy, such as heat, to a liquid, the particles speed up. At some point, the particles have so much energy that they break the force that holds them in a liquid state. The water vaporizes. **Vaporization** is the change of state from a liquid to a gas. Very fast vaporization is called boiling.

Slow or gradual vaporization is called **evaporation** (ih vap uh RAY shuhn). The higher the temperature, the faster evaporation will take place.

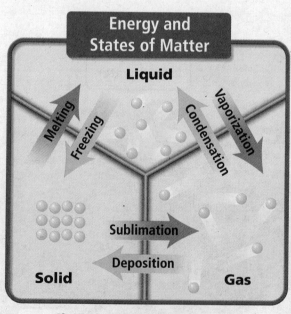

Changes in energy can cause changes in state.

Water vapor in the air condenses into liquid water on the outside of the cold bottle.

When energy is taken away from a gas, it will undergo condensation. **Condensation** (kahn dehn SAY shuhn) is a change of state from a gas to a liquid. It is the opposite of vaporization.

You can observe condensation on a very cold day. The air you breathe out has water vapor, which condenses when it loses energy to the cold air. That is why you can see your breath.

7. What causes condensation?

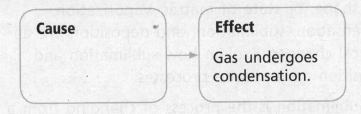

8. Look at the diagram on page 240. Find the changes that occur when a substance changes from a solid to a liquid or from a liquid to a gas. Circle the arrows that show that energy was added to cause these changes of state. Which arrows did you circle?

_____

_____

Summary   A physical change is a change in the size, shape, or state of matter. Vaporization, condensation, sublimation, and deposition are all physical changes. Explain how sublimation and deposition are opposite processes.

a. Sublimation is the process of changing from a

_____ directly to a _____.

b. Deposition is the process of changing from a

_____ directly to a _____.

⊚ Cause and Effect   What causes frost to form on windows?

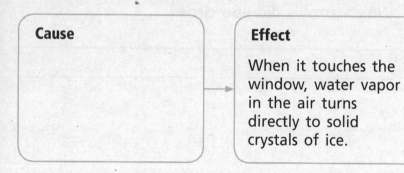

Cause	Effect
	When it touches the window, water vapor in the air turns directly to solid crystals of ice.

Skipping a Step

Sometimes, matter can skip the liquid state. When conditions are right, adding energy to a solid will change it directly to a gas. The process of changing from a solid to a gas is called **sublimation**. This is why dry ice is dry. It does not melt into a liquid, but sublimates into carbon dioxide gas.

The opposite of sublimation is deposition. Deposition is the change of state from a gas to a solid. Frost is a common example of deposition. When the temperature on windows or grass is below freezing, frost forms. When water vapor in the air touches one of these surfaces, it changes directly from a gas (water vapor) to a solid (ice).

DEPOSITION
When energy is removed from water vapor in the air, frost can be deposited on a freezing cold window.

CAUSE AND EFFECT

What causes frost to form on windows?

What Happens in a Chemical Reaction?

In a chemical change, chemical bonds are made or broken. This makes new substances. Chemical changes can either give off or absorb energy.

Forming New Substances

When a piece of matter changes physically, it keeps the same chemical makeup, or structure. But when a chemical change happens, there is a new substance with totally different particles than before. One group of substances becomes a new set of substances.

Inside a welding torch, a chemical change produces the energy needed to weld or cut metal.

VOCABULARY

product a substance that results from a chemical change *(noun)*

reactant a substance that enters into and is altered through the course of a chemical change *(noun)*

VOCABULARY SKILL: Word Origins

The word *product* comes from the Latin *producere*, which means "to bring forth." Use this information to explain what happens during a chemical change.

_____

_____

 1.a. Students know that chemical reactions result in products with different properties.
2.f. Students know how plants make food and release oxygen.

1. How is a chemical change different from a physical change?

_____

_____

_____

2. Put a check mark next to the items that are a sign that a chemical change has taken place.

_____ change in color

_____ release of heat

_____ change from a liquid to a gas

_____ change from a solid to a liquid

_____ release of light

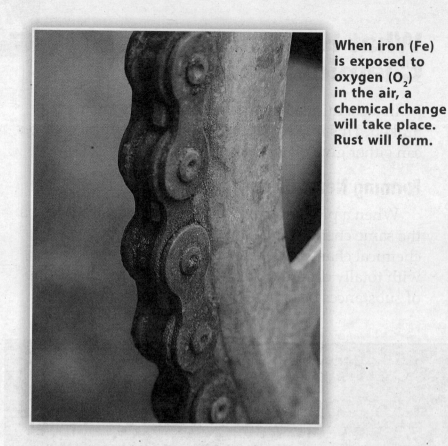

When iron (Fe) is exposed to oxygen (O_2) in the air, a chemical change will take place. Rust will form.

Examples of Chemical Changes

Chemical changes happen all around you every day. A change in color is one way to notice them. When a bicycle chain rusts, it turns a brown-red color. And when fruit ripens, which is also a chemical change, it changes color, too.

Some chemical changes happen quickly and give off a lot of light and heat. Burning wood is a good example of this. So is the chemical change that happens to gasoline in your car.

Other chemical changes happen slowly. Think of how your body has changed since you were little. Chemical changes are what make you grow.

Chemical Reactions

A chemical change is a change in which new substances are made. The substance that is changed during this process is called a **reactant**. The new substance that is made during the chemical change is called the **product**.

The force that holds atoms and molecules together is called a chemical bond. Chemical changes break those bonds and make new ones. This is what makes new substances with new chemical properties.

A chemical reaction is an example of a chemical change. The pictures below show chemical reactions.

Burning wood is an example of a chemical reaction.

When you twist a glow stick, you start a chemical reaction that produces a glowing light.

3. Circle the word that correctly completes each sentence.

   a. The substance that is changed during a chemical change is called a (reactant, product).

   b. The new substance that is made during a chemical change is called a (reactant, product).

4. Describe what happens during a chemical change.

   _____

   _____

   _____

245

5. How do scientists describe the reactants and products in a chemical reaction?

_____

6. Find the chemical equation at the bottom of the page. Label the reactants with an *R* and the products with a *P*.

Chemical Equations

Chemical equations are used by scientists to describe the reactants and products of a chemical reaction. The reactants, or the substances you start with, are on the left. On the right, after the arrow, are the products. The products are the new material made during the chemical change.

Sometimes scientists use the names of the substances in an equation. Most of the time, however, they use just the chemical formulas that represent the substances.

The chemical equation below shows that photosynthesis changes carbon dioxide and water into sugar and oxygen.

Carbon Dioxide	+ Water	$\longrightarrow$	Sugar	+ Oxygen
$6CO_2$	+ $6H_2O$	$\longrightarrow$	$C_6H_{12}O_6$	+ $6O_2$

Conservation of Matter

No matter what kind of change takes place, the amount of matter will always stay the same. Matter cannot be created or destroyed.

In some reactions it may look as if you got rid of some matter. If you burn a large pile of wood, what you are left with is just a small pile of ashes. But you did not destroy any matter. It just took on another form. In this case, the wood changes to gases, smoke, and ashes.

Chemical Change

ORIGINAL MATERIALS
Wood is mostly a carbon compound called cellulose. When heated, it will react with oxygen in the air.

CHEMICAL CHANGE
Cellulose and oxygen combine to form two gases: carbon dioxide and water vapor. The flames are hot, glowing gases.

NEW MATERIALS
Most of the wood has been changed into gases. Some carbon remains in ashes.

MAIN IDEA AND DETAILS

List three examples of chemical changes.

Summary A chemical change involves breaking some chemical bonds and making new bonds that form new substances. Chemical changes can either absorb or release energy.

Does the amount of matter change during physical and chemical changes? Why or why not?

_____

_____

Main Idea and Details List three examples of chemical changes.

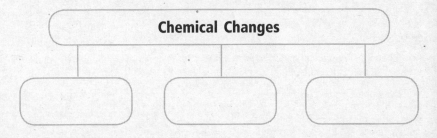

Chemical Changes

Glossary

Group two or more of the words in the glossary and explain why they go together.

Glossary

condensation (kahn dehn SAY shuhn) the change of state from a gas to a liquid

   condensación cambio de estado de gas a líquido

evaporation (ih VAP uh ray shuhn) the change in state from a liquid to a gas; slow or gradual vaporization

   evaporación cambio de estado de líquido a gas; vaporización lenta o gradual

gas a form of matter that has no definite shape or volume

   gas tipo de materia que no tiene forma o volumen definidos

liquid a form of matter that has a definite volume, but no definite shape

   líquido foma de materia que tiene volumen definido, pero no forma definida

mixture a physical combination of two or more substances

   mezcla combinación física de dos o más sustancias

product a substance that results from a chemical change

   producto sustancia que resulta de un cambio químico

Glossary

reactant a substance that enters into and is altered through the course of a chemical change

reactivo sustancia que entra en un cambio químico y se altera durante el transcurso del mismo

solid a form of matter that has a definite shape and volume

sólido estado de la materia que tiene forma y volumen definidos

solution a mixture in which parts are evenly distributed at the level of atoms or molecules

solución mezcla distribuida en partes iguales a nivel de átomos o moléculas

sublimation the process of a solid changing directly to a gas without passing through the liquid state

sublimación proceso por el cual un sólido pasa directamente a estado gaseoso sin pasar por el estado líquido

vaporization the process of a liquid changing into a gas

vaporización proceso por el cual un líquido cambia a gas

Visit www.eduplace.com to play puzzles and word games.

Circle the glossary term that is the same in both Spanish and English.

Chapter Review

WHAT DID YOU LEARN?

Think About What You Have Read

Vocabulary

❶ Circle the correct answer on the page.

Comprehension

❷ _____

❸ _____

❹ _____

   _____

Critical Thinking

❺ _____

   _____

   _____

   _____

Vocabulary

❶ The physical combination of two or more substances results in a/an _____.

   A) gas

   B) solution

   C) liquid

   D) mixture

Comprehension

❷ A substance that results from a chemical change is called a/an _____.

❸ A solution of two or more metals is a what?

❹ Is matter lost when wood burns?

Critical Thinking

❺ How are a solute and a solvent different?

Index